THE ONE GOAL
THE UNCOMPLICATED GUIDE TO SUCCESS

PATRICK RAYNE

Published by
Rupa Publications India Pvt. Ltd 2024
7/16, Ansari Road, Daryaganj
New Delhi 110002

Sales centres:
Bengaluru Chennai
Hyderabad Jaipur Kathmandu
Kolkata Mumbai Prayagraj

Copyright © Rupa Publications India Pvt. Ltd 2024

All rights reserved.
No part of this publication may be reproduced, transmitted,
or stored in a retrieval system, in any form or by any means,
electronic, mechanical, photocopying, recording or otherwise,
without the prior permission of the publisher.

P-ISBN: 978-93-6156-252-5
E-ISBN: 978-93-6156-922-7

First impression 2024

10 9 8 7 6 5 4 3 2 1

The moral right of the author has been asserted.

This book is sold subject to the condition that it shall not,
by way of trade or otherwise, be lent, resold, hired out, or otherwise
circulated, without the publisher's prior consent, in any form of
binding or cover other than that in which it is published.

Contents

1. The Epiphany — 1
2. The Butterfly Effect — 6
3. The Diverse Portfolio Theory — 13

PART ONE
THE MYTHS
THEY DISTRACT AND CONFUSE US

4. The Myth of Multitasking — 25
5. The Science Behind Task Switching — 29
6. Killer Habits of the Superstars — 44
7. Mindfulness: The True Power of Positivity — 55
8. The Palace of Stable Dreams — 76
9. Small Is the New Big: How Tiny Triumphs Make Life Gigantic — 88

PART TWO
RE-DETOX
THE VULNERABILITY ESSENTIALISM

10. Ask Away Anyway — 109
11. Fail Hard, Win Big: The Secret Sauce of Top Achievers — 114
12. Pause, Reflect and Just Chill — 121

PART THREE
THE LAW OF ATTRACTION
UNLOCKING YOUR INNER DREAMS

13. Crafting an Extraordinary Life	127
14. Celebrate Your Life	140
15. Nothing Doing	150
16. The Life Commandments	170
17. Extroverts, Introverts and Productivity	197
18. Revise and Refresh Your Mojo	221

1

The Epiphany

*Be like a river—keep flowing toward your goal,
overcoming every obstacle, until you reach the sea.*

—Inspired by Lao Tzu

I was failing. My life was in turmoil, and everything felt like it was falling apart. Despite all the dedication and hard work, my company, which we had built with national and international ambitions in less than a decade, was suddenly not working out. It wasn't until I hit this major roadblock that I began to connect my results with my approach.

I had experienced success in the past, but the true understanding came much later. The secret of success was delivered from the lips of a fictional character to my ears. Whether the writers knew it or stumbled upon it, the wisdom they wrote was pure truth. The ONE GOAL is the best approach to getting what you want.

In a memorable scene from the movie *City Slickers* (1991), Curly, played by Jack Palance, shares a moment of wisdom with Mitch, played by Billy Crystal. As they navigate life's challenges, Curly reveals his philosophy about the secret to life.

Curly: You know what the secret to life is?

Mitch: No, what?

Curly: This. [He holds up one finger.]

Mitch: Your finger?

Curly: One thing. Just one thing. You stick to that, and everything else doesn't mean shit.

Mitch: That's great, but what's the "one thing"?

Curly: That's what you've got to figure out.

This iconic scene in *City Slickers* became one of the most quoted moments from the film. It emphasizes the importance of finding a singular focus in life, leaving it to the individual to discover what that "one thing" is. This deeply motivational movie delivered life lessons through its emotionally charged scenes, resonating with viewers worldwide. I was completely engrossed in the film, and it was in that moment, amidst the audience's emotion and the movie's powerful message, that I began to see the connection between focus and success. That was the key secret that would change everything for me.

That was—THE KEY SECRET—my epiphany moment!

The Final Straw

And suddenly, it all clicked. The student remembered his successes and failures and discovered an interesting pattern. When he'd had huge success, he had narrowed his concentration to one goal, and where his success varied, his focus had too.

Teacher: Look at your results now. They went through the roof, didn't they?

Student: Yes, they did. After you asked, "What's the ONE GOAL you can do this week such that by doing it everything else would be easier or unnecessary?" something incredible happened.

Teacher: Sometimes, out of desperation, we need to go as small as possible. I remember shortening your list from three things to two things, and finally to just one.

Student: And that's when everything changed. When I focused on just one task, the outcome was extraordinary.

Teacher: You've found your key focus now. But remember, this is just the beginning. Having found your 14 key tasks, you need to continue working with precision.

Student: Yes, I've started working on building my skills and tasks individually. I used to make a long list of things to do, but most of them didn't matter much.

Teacher: Exactly. So, in an effort to help you succeed, I started shortening your list. It's all about the ONE GOAL now.

Student: This approach has led to extraordinary success. In just three years, I've seen sustained growth and improvement in my studies.

Teacher: And this is how you grow from a regional achiever to an international contender. Now, let's talk about how you got here.

Student: Well, I remember the day I decided to fire myself. *It was a huge decision, but it was clearly the MOST important thing I could do.*

Teacher: It was a transformational moment for you. Sometimes, we have to consider how a few changes can make a big difference. With the right focus, you saw radical changes in your performance and life.

Student: I remember our first discussion. You asked me a simple question, "Do you know what you need to do to turn things around?"

Teacher: And you hadn't a clue. That's when we started this journey together.

Student: You had my organizational chart up on the wall. Your research was thorough. You helped me revisit my goals.

Teacher: With a full grasp of the issues, we set out in search of answers. I walked you through your situation and the challenges you faced, both personal and academic.

Student: Seeking help from you was the best decision I made.

Mastering Minimalism: The Art of Essential Focus

The law of attraction aligns perfectly with a focused approach, magnetizing **success** by channelling your energy to the pivotal areas. When you narrow your scope to what truly matters, you find yourself directly aligned with your true objectives. This is not just a method but a philosophy that consistently delivers **extraordinary results**. This streamlined path to success keeps you devoted to the essentials.

Real accumulation of **outcomes** is about minimizing efforts rather than expanding them. You have limited time and energy; spreading yourself too thin reduces your impact. This minimalist strategy sidesteps common pitfalls of overcommitment—like stress, burnout, and missed moments with loved ones—facilitating a smoother, quicker path to realizing your goals.

The most efficient way to enhance both your professional and personal spheres is to reduce complexities as much as possible. In contradiction to popular belief, grand success is born not from convoluted or lengthy endeavors but from mastering a few selected tasks. While many struggle with an overload of work leading to minimal accomplishments, true success is rooted in selectivity—accomplishing more with fewer, focused efforts.

Core Distinctions in Focusing Your Efforts

- Identify and focus on the **vital few** tasks, ignoring the trivial many.
- Recognize that not all tasks are equal; some have the potential to impact greatly while others might not.
- Realize that **exceptional outcomes** are directly determined by how narrowly you can channel your focus.

By embracing the essence of going **compact**, you dismiss a plethora of options and concentrate on the necessities. It's about honing in on the indispensable few tasks. This method ensures a deep connection between your actions and your dreams, acknowledging that outstanding results are crafted by how intensely you can channel your energies.

Harnessing Focus: The Power of Minimalism

Everyone is allotted the same 24 hours each day, yet the variance in what individuals achieve is vast. The secret to heightened success, enhanced earnings, and richer experiences is their adept strategy of focusing intensely on the most impactful tasks. They prioritize simplicity.

Remember, the river flows steadily to the sea, overcoming every obstacle. Your focus will guide you through challenges and lead you to your ultimate success. Stay focused, stay dedicated, and let the power of minimalism drive you forward.

2

The Butterfly Effect

Making something and sending it out into the world and then people not only responding to it but adopting it for their own and making a separate thing for it, that's beautiful. It just shows you how much you can affect other people... the butterfly effect of everything you put out into the world.

—Marketa Irglova

Tiny Actions, Big Ripples

In chaos theory, **the Butterfly Effect** is the idea that small changes in initial conditions can lead to vastly different outcomes. Imagine a butterfly flapping its wings in Brazil, setting off a chain of events that culminates in a tornado in Texas. This concept illustrates how seemingly insignificant actions can have monumental impacts, emphasizing the power of minute influences.

The Legendary Butterfly Flap

Let's take a fascinating anecdote from 1961 when meteorologist **Edward Lorenz** stumbled upon this concept. While running a weather simulation, he rounded off a number from 0.506127 to

0.506, expecting negligible changes. However, the result was a drastically different weather pattern. This discovery highlighted the sensitivity of complex systems to initial conditions and gave birth to the term "Butterfly Effect."

Small Changes, Big Differences

Just as one butterfly can alter the weather, small, deliberate actions can create **extraordinary results** in our lives. Here's a closer look at how the Butterfly Effect works in different areas:

Personal Development

- **Learning a New Skill**: Consider the story of renowned pianist Lang Lang. He didn't start by playing concertos; he began with simple scales and exercises. Each practice session, no matter how small, contributed to his mastery.
- **Building Habits**: *James Clear*, author of *Atomic Habits*, explains that small, consistent habits compound over time. Imagine improving by just 1 per cent every day. While it may seem insignificant initially, these small gains lead to a 37-times improvement by the end of the year.

Health and Fitness

- **Nutrition**: Adopting healthier eating habits can start with a single change, like swapping soda for water. Over time, this small shift can lead to significant health improvements, including weight loss and better metabolic health.
- **Exercise**: Starting with just a few minutes of daily exercise can snowball into a robust fitness routine. Many successful athletes began their journeys with modest, consistent efforts.

Career Success

- **Networking:** A single, well-placed email or attending a networking event can open doors to new career opportunities. These small actions can lead to significant professional growth.
- **Skill Development:** Investing a few minutes each day to learn a new skill, like coding or public speaking, can exponentially enhance your career prospects.

The Snowball Effect: Inspirational Stories

The Butterfly Effect is akin to a **snowball rolling down a hill**. It starts small but gathers momentum, growing larger and more powerful. Let's delve into a few real-life examples:

The Birth of Google

In 1996, two Stanford students, **Larry Page and Sergey Brin**, embarked on a small research project. Their goal was to improve internet search capabilities. This small initiative led to the creation of Google, which revolutionized the internet and became a cornerstone of the digital age.

The Wright Brothers' First Flight

In 1903, **Orville and Wilbur Wright** achieved the first powered flight with a modest, 12-second airborne adventure. This small step marked the beginning of aviation, transforming transportation and connecting the world.

The Story of J.K. Rowling

Before becoming a world-famous author, J.K. Rowling was an unemployed single mother. A small decision to start writing her ideas on paper in a coffee shop led to the creation of the Harry Potter series, a global phenomenon that has inspired millions.

The Rise of Airbnb

In 2007, two struggling entrepreneurs, Brian Chesky and Joe Gebbia, decided to rent out air mattresses in their apartment to make some extra money. This small act of resourcefulness eventually grew into Airbnb, a billion-dollar company that has revolutionized the travel industry.

The Hong Kong-Dollar Crisis

In 1997, a slight change in interest rates by the Federal Reserve caused a massive ripple effect that led to the collapse of the Hong Kong dollar. This event demonstrated how a small financial decision in one part of the world could have catastrophic economic consequences elsewhere.

The Assassination of Archduke Franz Ferdinand

Another historical example is the assassination of Archduke Franz Ferdinand of Austria in 1914. This single event, which seemed minor at the time, set off a series of alliances and conflicts that led to World War I, changing the course of history forever.

Creating Your Own Butterfly Effect

Personal development is heavily influenced by the Butterfly Effect. Implementing small, positive habits can lead to significant improvements over time.

Set Small, Achievable Goals

- **Daily Micro-Tasks:** Break down large goals into tiny, manageable tasks. Completing these micro-tasks consistently leads to substantial progress.

- **Celebrate Small Wins**: Recognize and celebrate minor achievements. This reinforces positive behaviour and keeps motivation high.

Prioritize Consistency Over Intensity

- **Routine Building**: Establishing a routine ensures that small actions become habits. Consistency is more powerful than sporadic, intense efforts.
- **Incremental Improvements**: Focus on making incremental improvements rather than drastic changes. This approach is sustainable and less overwhelming.

The Ripple Effect: Extending the Butterfly Effect

Small actions impact the immediate environment and create a **ripple effect**, influencing others and extending far beyond the initial action.

Acts of Kindness

- **Pay It Forward**: Simple acts of kindness, like helping a neighbour or complimenting a colleague, can inspire others to do the same. This creates a chain reaction of positivity.
- **Community Impact**: Volunteering a few hours at a local charity can inspire others to contribute, amplifying the overall impact on the community.

Environmental Stewardship

- **Sustainable Practices**: Adopting eco-friendly habits, such as recycling or reducing energy consumption, encourages others to follow suit, collectively making a significant environmental impact.
- **Advocacy**: Advocating for sustainable policies, even on a

small scale, can lead to broader changes in legislation and corporate practices.

The Future Impact: Small Innovations Leading to Major Advancements

History is replete with examples of small innovations leading to major advancements. Consider the following:

Technological Breakthroughs

- **The Microchip**: The development of the microchip in the 1950s was a small innovation with profound implications, laying the foundation for modern computing and electronics.
- **The Internet**: Originally a small research project funded by the US Department of Defense, the internet has transformed every aspect of society, from communication to commerce.

Medical Advances

- **Penicillin**: Discovered by Alexander Fleming in 1928, penicillin was a small accident. It has since saved millions of lives and revolutionized medicine.
- **Vaccines**: The development of vaccines, often starting with small, incremental research efforts, has eradicated diseases like smallpox and continues to protect global health.

Harnessing the Butterfly Effect for Positive Change

Environmental Initiatives

Individuals and communities can harness the Butterfly Effect to drive environmental change. **Simple actions like recycling, reducing energy consumption and supporting sustainable**

practices can collectively lead to significant environmental benefits.

Social Movements

Social movements often start with small actions. **The civil rights movement began with individual acts of defiance** and grew into a powerful force for change. Today, social media amplifies these small actions, allowing movements to gain momentum and influence rapidly.

Embrace the Power of Small Actions

The Butterfly Effect teaches us that small actions can have monumental impacts. Whether in science, technology, personal development or social change, recognizing the power of tiny changes can help us make more informed decisions and inspire us to take those first small steps toward achieving extraordinary results.

By understanding and embracing the Butterfly Effect, we can unlock the potential for positive change in our lives and the world around us. So, **next time you encounter a small decision, remember its potential to create a ripple effect** that could lead to something truly remarkable.

3

The Diverse Portfolio Theory

> *Coming together is a beginning, staying together is progress, and working together is success.*
>
> —Henry Ford

This theory posits that companies should focus on diversifying their products and services to achieve sustained success. Rather than concentrating on one key product or service, companies should develop multiple strong offerings to create a balanced and resilient portfolio. This approach is based on the idea that diversification reduces risk, allows for cross-promotion, and can cater to a broader range of consumer needs.

Multi-Product, Multi-Service Strategy

The core idea of the Diverse Portfolio theory is that successful companies thrive by offering a variety of products and services. This strategy helps to mitigate risks and leverage cross-market opportunities. For instance, Amazon started as an online bookstore but quickly diversified into selling a multitude of products and services, including cloud computing, video streaming and artificial intelligence (AI). This diverse portfolio has made Amazon a resilient and dominant player in multiple industries.

Risk Mitigation

Diversification helps companies spread risk. If one product fails or a market shifts, other products or services can sustain the company. Consider Procter & Gamble, which owns a vast array of brands across various consumer goods sectors. If one product line underperforms, the success of others can offset the impact, ensuring the company's overall stability.

Cross-Promotion and Synergy

A diverse portfolio allows for cross-promotion and the creation of synergies between different products and services. Microsoft, for example, benefits from the integration of its software, hardware and cloud services, creating a cohesive ecosystem that enhances user experience and loyalty. By offering a range of complementary products, companies can create added value for their customers.

Adapting to Market Changes

Companies with a diverse portfolio are better positioned to adapt to market changes and emerging trends. For instance, General Electric (GE) operates in multiple sectors, including aviation, healthcare, and renewable energy. This diversification enables GE to pivot and invest in growing industries while maintaining a presence in established markets.

Example of Successful Diversification

1. **Sony Corporation**: Sony is known for its diverse range of products, including electronics, gaming, entertainment and

financial services. This diversification has allowed Sony to remain competitive and innovative across various sectors.
2. **Johnson & Johnson**: With a portfolio that spans pharmaceuticals, medical devices and consumer health products, Johnson & Johnson has built a robust business model that leverages its expertise across different healthcare segments.

While focusing on a single product or service can lead to extraordinary success, the Diverse Portfolio theory suggests that building a broad and varied range of offerings can create a more resilient and adaptable business. Companies that embrace diversification can better withstand market fluctuations, reduce risk, and capitalize on multiple growth opportunities, ultimately achieving long-term success.

Do not put all your eggs in one basket.

—Warren Buffett

One Company, Multiple Heroes

Just as the Diverse Portfolio approach applies to products and services, it also applies to the people within a company. Instead of relying on one key person, businesses can build a team of individuals who each bring unique strengths to the table. This collective effort drives the company forward more effectively.

Take the example of Apple. Steve Jobs is often credited with the company's success, but he was supported by a talented team, including co-founder Steve Wozniak, design guru Jony Ive and operations expert Tim Cook. Each brought something different to the table, and together they propelled Apple to new heights.

No One Succeeds Alone

In the Diverse Portfolio theory, success is a team effort. Consider Pixar Animation Studios. While John Lasseter is often highlighted as a driving force behind Pixar's success, the studio's achievements are the result of a collaborative effort involving talented animators, writers, directors and producers. Each project benefits from the collective skills and creativity of the team.

Multiple Passions, Multiple Skills

Successful individuals often excel in multiple areas, leveraging a variety of passions and skills to achieve extraordinary results. This multi-faceted approach can lead to a richer and more resilient career path.

> *Don't be afraid to give up*
> *the good to go for the great.*
>
> —John D. Rockefeller

Consider Elon Musk. His diverse interests and skills have led him to found and lead multiple successful ventures, including Tesla, SpaceX, Neuralink and The Boring Company. By applying his talents across various industries, Musk has created a diversified portfolio of businesses that collectively contribute to his success.

Passion Leads to Skill, and Skill Leads to Success

Passion and skill often go hand in hand. As individuals dedicate time to their passions, they naturally develop the skills needed to excel. This, in turn, leads to better results, more enjoyment, and further investment in their passions.

Take the story of Arnold Schwarzenegger. His passion for bodybuilding led him to become Mr Olympia, his skill in acting made him a Hollywood star, and his interest in politics propelled him to become the Governor of California. Each success was built on the foundation of his diverse passions and skills.

One Life, Multiple Paths

A diversified approach to life can lead to extraordinary fulfillment and success. By embracing various interests and opportunities, individuals can create a rich tapestry of experiences that contribute to their overall well-being.

Look at Richard Branson. His life's work spans numerous industries, from music with Virgin Records to aviation with Virgin Atlantic, and even space travel with Virgin Galactic. Each venture adds a new dimension to his legacy, showcasing the power of a diversified life.

A Diversified Legacy

The Diverse Portfolio approach can extend to philanthropy and social impact. Bill and Melinda Gates, through their foundation, tackle various global challenges, from health and education to poverty alleviation. Their diversified focus allows them to address multiple issues effectively, leveraging different strategies and solutions to create a broad and lasting impact.

Multiple Locations, Multiple Markets

Another aspect of the Diverse Portfolio theory is geographical diversification. Companies that expand their operations into various regions and markets can reduce dependency on any single market and better manage global economic fluctuations. For example, McDonald's operates in over 100 countries, adapting its menu to cater to local tastes while maintaining its core offerings. This geographical diversity helps McDonald's stabilize its revenue streams and capitalize on growth opportunities in different regions.

One Vision, Multiple Strategies

A diverse portfolio doesn't mean lacking focus. Companies with a broad range of products and services often have a unified vision that guides their multiple strategies. Google, for instance, started with search but has diversified into advertising, cloud computing, hardware and AI. Despite the diversity, the unifying vision of organizing the world's information and making it universally accessible and useful ties all its endeavours together.

Multiple Streams Of Innovation

Innovation can come from various sources within a diversified company. Take 3M, known for its culture of innovation and wide array of products. From Post-it notes to industrial adhesives, 3M encourages its employees to spend a portion of their time on projects outside their regular work. This approach has led to a steady stream of innovative products across different industries.

PART ONE

THE MYTHS
They Distract and Confuse Us

Change is the end result of all true learning.

—Leo Buscaglia

When Yesterday Overstays Its Welcome

Alright folks, buckle up! We're diving into the crazy carnival of life, where our brains love to juggle with old, wacky beliefs, even when they're as wrong as thinking a pineapple is a great hat. This makes sticking to the one goal feel like trying to focus on a single cat in a room full of laser pointers. Our minds get tangled in a jungle of mixed-up ideas, throwing us off course and making success as elusive as finding a needle in a haystack, blindfolded.

Life's too short to be chasing unicorns and relying on lucky rabbits's feet. Real answers are often right under our noses, hidden by a noisy parade of myths and so-called "common sense" that's about as sensible as wearing socks with sandals. Think about it: The myth that a frog won't jump out of slowly heated water? Total baloney. Or the idea that fish rots from the head down? Utter fishy nonsense. Success myths are no different: the lie that you must be perfect at everything, that constant hustling is the secret sauce, or that it's too late to start fresh. These six success myths are like kryptonite to The Only Thing. To really win, we need to spot these myths, toss them in the bin, and keep moving forward, all while being aware of their sneaky ways.

Flashback to 2023, when Merriam-Webster crowned "authentic" as the Word of the Year. Why? Because being true to yourself has become the ultimate superpower! Lookups for this word skyrocketed thanks to chatter about AI, celebrity antics, personal identity and the social media circus. Authenticity, meaning "not fake or imitation" and "true to one's own personality, spirit, or character," was the year's hot topic. Even celebs like Taylor Swift were on a quest to find their "authentic voice." As AI blurred the lines between real and fake, being authentic became a show in itself, with "authentic content creators" turning into the new trust heroes.

Our world often feels like it's been yanked straight from a dystopian novel. The year 2023 gave us AI-generated nightmarish scenarios, record-breaking heat waves and smoke-filled skies from wildfires. The fear of AI turning us into its minions only added fuel to the dystopian fire, making it more crucial than ever to find our own sunshine amidst the gloom.

Then there's the term "doppelgänger," which grabbed our attention, pointing to lookalikes or evil twins. Stories of crimes and media spins made us fascinated yet creeped out by these doubles. It's a strong nudge to avoid becoming someone's carbon copy and to celebrate our unique quirks.

And let's not forget "elemental," brought back into the spotlight by Pixar's *Elemental*. The film's use of classical elements—air, water, fire and earth—as metaphors for identity and bias nudged us to stay true to our roots, own our choices, and embrace our core selves. With these wisdom nuggets, we're inspired to value authenticity, challenge dystopian vibes, resist being copycats, and celebrate our elemental selves.

Life, this wild rollercoaster ride, is a patchwork of realness, challenges and wins. By ditching the misconceptions and embracing our true selves, we tap into endless potential. Success isn't about endless grinding or chasing perfection but about genuinely following our passions and standing firm in our truths. So, grab life by the horns, be your true self, and let your inner light shine bright every step of the way. Be bold, be authentic, and let your real self light up your path!

The Six Secrets No One Will Tell You

1. Perfection Is Key
2. Hustle Culture
3. Solitary Achievement
4. Talent Trumps All
5. Total Sacrifice
6. Too Late to Start

These six are beliefs that lodge themselves in our minds and become guiding principles that lead us astray. They are roads that end in dead ends, fool's gold that distracts us from true wealth. If we're to reach our full potential, we need to debunk these myths and lay them to rest.

1. Perfection Is Key

> *Have no fear of perfection—you'll never reach it.*
>
> —Salvador Dalí

The belief that everything must be perfect before you can proceed is a myth that stalls progress. Perfectionism can paralyse you, causing missed opportunities and endless procrastination. Striving for excellence is commendable, but expecting perfection can be detrimental. Embrace imperfection as part of the journey and understand that progress often comes from trial and error, not flawless execution.

2. Hustle Culture

The idea that success only comes from constant, relentless hustle is misleading. While hard work is important, the glorification of busyness leads to burnout and diminishes productivity. Balance and strategic rest are crucial for maintaining long-term success.

Work smarter, not harder, and recognize that effective time management and prioritization often yield better results than perpetual hustle.

> *You can't have a million-dollar dream*
> *with a minimum-wage work ethic.*

—Stephen C. Hogan

3. Solitary Achievement

The myth that you must do it all yourself to succeed is a common misconception. Success is rarely a solo endeavour; it's built on collaboration, mentorship and support networks. Surround yourself with people who can offer guidance, share the load, and provide different perspectives. Building a strong team and seeking help when needed are vital components of sustainable success.

4. Talent Trumps All

Believing that only those with innate talent can achieve great things overlooks the importance of persistence, hard work and continuous learning. Talent can give you a head start, but it's the consistent effort and willingness to grow that ultimately lead to success. Cultivate a growth mindset and focus on developing your skills and knowledge, regardless of where you start.

5. Total Sacrifice

The notion that you must sacrifice everything—health, relationships, personal interests—to achieve success is a damaging myth. True success encompasses a balanced life where personal well-being and meaningful connections are maintained. Neglecting these aspects can lead to regret and a hollow sense of achievement. Prioritize self-care and nurture relationships to ensure a well-rounded, fulfilling life.

6. Too Late to Start

The belief that it's too late to pursue your dreams or make a significant change is a myth that stifles potential. Age and timing are often used as excuses to avoid taking risks or stepping out of comfort zones. The truth is, it's never too late to start something new or make a pivot in your career or personal life. Embrace change and take action, regardless of your age or circumstances.

Debunking the Myths

Recognizing these myths is the first step towards achieving genuine success. By letting go of these false beliefs, you clear the path to focus on what truly matters. Embrace a mindset that values progress over perfection, balance over busyness, collaboration over isolation, effort over innate talent, holistic success over total sacrifice, and bold action over hesitation.

The Truth about Success

Success isn't about adhering to rigid myths; it's about finding what works for you and continually adapting. Here are some guiding principles to replace the myths:

1. **Embrace Imperfection**: Aim for progress, not perfection. Each step forward, no matter how small, is a victory.
2. **Balance Work and Rest**: Recognize the importance of rest and recovery. Sustainable success comes from a well-rested mind and body.
3. **Build a Support Network**: Seek collaboration and mentorship. Together, we achieve more.

4

The Myth of Multitasking

*The main thing is to keep the
main thing the main thing.*

—Stephen Covey

Multitasking

The belief that we can effectively juggle multiple tasks at once is pervasive in a world that celebrates multitasking. However, science tells us a different story: the human brain isn't wired to handle several activities simultaneously without a cost. Multitasking is a myth.

Understanding this is crucial for effective decision-making.

*There is nothing so useless as doing efficiently
that which should not be done at all.*

—Peter Drucker

When everything seems urgent, we default to multitasking, believing it's the answer to managing our workload. We switch from one task to another, thinking we're making progress. But in reality, we're trading efficiency for inefficiency. The result is a day filled with activity but lacking in true productivity.

We respond when we don't have a clear plan for setting priorities. Our choices are based on preconceived notions, which make us do things without much thought. This impulsive way of doing things hurts our chances of success, like a scary movie character who always does the wrong thing. We often settle for any choice instead of the best one, and instead of moving forward, we get stuck in a loop of being busy.

When every task feels equally urgent and important, we become trapped in a false sense of productivity. Activity doesn't equal achievement, and busyness rarely equates to meaningful progress.

> *Most people fail in life because they major in minor things.*
>
> —Tony Robbins

Knocking out a hundred inconsequential tasks is a poor substitute for focusing on one significant task. Multitasking gives the illusion of productivity but often results in diluted efforts and subpar results.

The Truth about Focus

Recognizing the myth of multitasking is the first step toward achieving real success. Here are some principles to help you focus on what truly matters:

1. **Single-Tasking**: Focus on one task at a time. Give it your full attention and complete it before moving on to the next. This approach improves the quality of your work and reduces errors.
2. **Prioritization**: Determine what's most important. Use tools like the Eisenhower Matrix to differentiate between urgent

and important tasks. Prioritize tasks that align with your long-term goals.
3. **Time Blocking**: Allocate specific time slots for different activities. Protect these blocks from interruptions to maintain deep focus and productivity.
4. **Mindful Work**: Be present in your tasks. Mindfulness reduces stress and enhances concentration, leading to better performance.
5. **Rest and Recovery**: Schedule breaks to rest your mind. Continuous work without breaks leads to burnout and decreased productivity. Use techniques like the Pomodoro Technique to balance work and rest.

Shifting from multitasking to focused, mindful work can increase productivity and success. Let go of the myth of multitasking and embrace the power of prioritization and single-tasking. This approach enhances efficiency and ensures meaningful progress toward goals.

The Journey of Discovery

Dr Santos often reflected on the winding path that had led her to this moment. "Science," she would say, "is not a straight line. It's a journey filled with unexpected turns and uncharted territories." She recalled her early days as a graduate student, working late into the night in the lab, driven by a relentless curiosity and a passion for understanding the universe.

One evening, while poring over data, she had an epiphany. "It was like a light bulb went off in my head," she recounted. "I realized that I had been spreading myself too thin, trying to tackle too many questions at once. That's when I decided to focus on just one hypothesis—the nature of dark matter."

Her decision to concentrate on dark matter was not without its challenges. She faced scepticism from some of her peers, who believed that diversifying her research would yield more results. But Dr Santos remained steadfast. "I knew that if I could make a breakthrough in understanding dark matter, it would be worth more than a hundred smaller discoveries."

5

The Science Behind Task Switching

It is not enough to be busy. So are the ants.
The question is: What are we busy about?

—Henry David Thoreau

Thoreau's quote emphasizes the importance of being mindful of what we are dedicating our time and energy to, highlighting that mere busyness is not equivalent to productivity. This aligns perfectly with the idea that task switching, while it may make us feel busy, often results in inefficiency and reduced effectiveness.

A Cognitive Circus

Our minds are perpetually teeming with activity, with thousands of thoughts streaming through our consciousness daily. This relentless mental traffic often convinces us that multitasking is an essential skill. We pride ourselves on managing numerous responsibilities at once—whether at work, at home or in our personal lives. However, switching our focus every few seconds is like attempting to herd cats; it's disorderly and ultimately ineffective.

Evolutionary Necessity

The concept of multitasking is deeply embedded in our evolutionary history. Our ancestors had to juggle multiple tasks for survival, like scanning for predators while foraging for food or tanning hides. This ability to oversee numerous activities simultaneously was crucial for their existence. They couldn't afford to lose focus while gathering berries or sitting by the fire after a long day of hunting. This multitasking trait is a survival mechanism that has been passed down through generations. As Socrates aptly put it, "The secret of change is to focus all your energy not on fighting the old but on building the new."

The Trickster's Balancing Act

At first glance, the balancing appears to be a perfect example of multitasking. To the observer, a juggler seems to manage several balls at once. In reality, they are catching and tossing each ball in rapid succession—one at a time. This is what researchers call "task switching." True focus, much like juggling, involves handling one task at a time. Peter Drucker once remarked, "Efficiency is doing things right; effectiveness is doing the right things."

This distinction is crucial in understanding why multitasking fails us. Efficiency focuses on performing tasks in the most economical manner, while effectiveness is about ensuring that we are focusing on the right tasks. When we try to juggle multiple activities simultaneously, we may become efficient in handling minor, low-impact tasks, but we lose sight of the larger, more important objectives. The frequent switching of attention fragments our efforts, causing us to miss critical details and make errors that we wouldn't make if we were fully focused.

Consider the scenario of working on a detailed financial report while intermittently checking emails and answering phone calls. Each interruption diverts your concentration, leading to mistakes in your calculations or oversights in the data. By the end of the day, you may have responded to all your emails and calls, but the quality and accuracy of your report suffer. This illustrates Drucker's point: Multitasking may create an illusion of productivity, but true effectiveness requires a dedicated focus on one significant task at a time.

Furthermore, the mental strain that comes from switching between tasks on a regular basis can lead to cognitive fatigue, which in turn reduces our general capacity to do even the most basic of tasks well. Studies have shown that it can take several minutes to regain our full cognitive function after an interruption. In the long run, this not only hampers our productivity but also increases stress levels, impacting our mental and physical health.

To achieve true effectiveness, it is essential to prioritize tasks based on their importance and potential impact. By focusing on one task at a time and completing it to the best of our ability, we can ensure that we are not just doing things right, but doing the right things. This approach aligns with the wisdom of both Bruce Lee and Peter Drucker, emphasizing the power of concentrated effort and mindful attention in achieving success and productivity.

> *The successful warrior is the average man*
> *with laser-like focus.*
>
> —Bruce Lee

Bruce Lee underscores the power of concentrated effort. Just as the average person can achieve greatness through focused attention, avoiding the pitfalls of multitasking can lead to greater productivity and success.

The Hidden Costs of Task Switching

Every time you switch from one task to another, whether voluntarily or not, you incur a cost. The first cost is the decision to switch, which happens almost instantly. The second cost is less predictable—it involves activating the "rules" for the new task. For simple tasks, like watching television and folding clothes, this switch is quick and painless. However, for more complex tasks, such as working on a spreadsheet and then discussing a business problem with a colleague, the cost is much higher. The time it takes to switch can increase by over 100 per cent for complicated tasks.

Our brains are equipped with different channels to process various types of data. This is why you can walk and talk at the same time without interference. However, when two tasks require focus from the same channel, problems arise. For instance, if you're trying to talk a passenger through landing a plane, you'd stop walking. Similarly, if you were crossing a rope bridge over a gorge, you'd likely stop talking to focus on your balance. Genuine focus shines a spotlight on a single task, leaving others in the dark. Alexander Graham Bell captured this well when he said, "Concentrate all your thoughts upon the work at hand. The sun's rays do not burn until brought to a focus."

The Pitfalls of Divided Attention

Dividing your attention between multiple tasks dilutes your effectiveness. When you attempt to focus on more than one important task at the same time, the quality of your work suffers. This is particularly true when one task demands more attention or uses a channel already in use. For example, if your spouse is describing how the living room furniture has been rearranged while you're driving, your visual cortex engages to visualize the arrangement. This channel interference can make you blind to the car braking in front of you. Albert E.N. Gray's wisdom rings true here: "The successful person has the habit of doing the things failures don't like to do."

Multitasking Inefficiencies

Multitasking not only leads to inefficiencies and mistakes but also increases stress. Embracing focused attention can enhance productivity and overall well-being. As Tim Ferriss advises, "Focus on being productive instead of busy." Here's a short list of how multitasking short-circuits us:

Impact of Multitasking on Different Aspects of Life

Cognitive and Brain Function

1. **Limited Brain Capacity**:
   o **Description**: Our brains can only handle so much at once. When we spread ourselves too thin, we sacrifice both time and efficiency.
   o **Affected Groups**:
     - Working Professionals
     - Students
     - Creative Minds
2. **Distorted Perception**:
   o **Description**: Chronic multitaskers often misjudge how long tasks truly take, typically believing they require more time than necessary.
   o **Affected Groups**:

- Working Professionals
- Managers
- Project Planners

3. **Lost Time**:
   - **Description**: Jumping from one task to another causes our brains to reset, wasting precious moments. Studies show we lose about 28 per cent of our workday to the inefficiency of multitasking.
   - **Affected Groups**:
     - Working Professionals
     - Students
     - Entrepreneurs

4. **Reduced Memory Retention**:
   - **Description**: Constantly switching tasks affects our memory. We're less likely to retain information accurately, leading to gaps in knowledge and understanding.
   - **Affected Groups**:
     - Students
     - Working Professionals
     - Researchers

5. **Impaired Learning**:
   - **Description**: Multitasking while learning new skills or absorbing new information diminishes our ability to fully grasp and retain the material, making the learning process less effective.
   - **Affected Groups**:
     - Students
     - Trainees
     - Lifelong Learners

Professional and Work Performance

1. **Disrupted Flow:**
   - **Description:** The more frequently we switch tasks, the harder it becomes to return to our original activity. This leads to unfinished projects piling up.
   - **Affected Groups:**
     - Working Professionals
     - Freelancers
     - Creative Minds

2. **Increased Errors:**
   - **Description:** Those who multitask tend to make more mistakes and poorer decisions, often favoring new, less relevant information over valuable older data.
   - **Affected Groups:**
     - Working Professionals
     - Quality Assurance Analysts
     - Managers

3. **Lowered Quality of Work:**
   - **Description:** As we spread our attention across multiple tasks, the quality of our work suffers. Attention to detail is compromised, leading to subpar results.
   - **Affected Groups:**
     - Creative Professionals
     - Engineers
     - Healthcare Workers

4. **Decreased Creativity:**
   - **Description:** Multitasking hampers our ability to think creatively. When our attention is divided, we struggle to make innovative connections and develop new ideas.

- **Affected Groups**:
  - Artists
  - Writers
  - Designers

Personal and Emotional Well-Being

1. **Heightened Stress**:
   - **Description**: Multitasking leads to elevated stress levels, eroding our happiness and overall well-being.
   - **Affected Groups**:
     - Everyone
2. **Negative Impact on Relationships**:
   - **Description**: Multitasking in personal interactions, like checking your phone during a conversation, can lead to weakened relationships. People may feel undervalued and disconnected when they don't receive our full attention.
   - **Affected Groups**:
     - Family Members
     - Friends
     - Colleagues
3. **Mental Fatigue**:
   - **Description**: The mental strain of constant task switching can lead to cognitive exhaustion, reducing our overall capacity to perform even simple tasks effectively.
   - **Affected Groups**:
     - Working Professionals
     - Students
     - Caregivers

4. **Decreased Satisfaction**:
   o **Description**: Focusing on multiple tasks at once can lead to a sense of dissatisfaction, as tasks are often completed with less quality and less fulfillment.
   o **Affected Groups**:
     - Working Professionals
     - Creative Minds
     - Students
5. **Lack of Presence**:
   o **Description**: Constant multitasking can make it difficult to be present in the moment, affecting mindfulness and enjoyment of daily activities.
   o **Affected Groups**:
     - Everyone

Sequential Task Management

Approach: Prioritize and Tackle One Task at a Time

Imagine you're a chef preparing a multi-course meal. Each dish requires your undivided attention. Here's how sequential task management works:

Chef Maria's Culinary Symphony: Chef Maria orchestrates a dinner service. She starts with appetizers, ensuring each plate is perfect. Only then does she move on to entrées. By focusing on one course at a time, she delivers an exquisite dining experience.

Batch Processing

Approach: Group Similar Tasks and Work Consecutively

Meet Alex, a content creator managing social media, emails, and content creation:

Alex's Content Creation Marathon: Alex batches tasks. In the morning, he crafts social media posts—writing, editing and scheduling them together. Then, he dives into email responses. By grouping similar activities, Alex minimizes context switching and maintains his creative flow.

Time Blocking

Approach: Allocate Specific Time Blocks for Different Activities

Picture Sarah, a project manager balancing meetings, reports and team coordination:

Sarah's Time-Blocked Calendar: Sarah designates morning hours for meetings, afternoons for report analysis and late evenings for brainstorming. During each block, she immerses herself in the designated task. Her structured approach minimizes distractions and boosts productivity.

Deep Work Sessions

Approach: Set Aside Uninterrupted Focused Work Periods

Imagine Mark, a software developer aiming for code mastery:

Mark's Code Crafting Retreat: Mark schedules deep work sessions. He silences notifications, closes unnecessary tabs, and dives into complex coding challenges. During these uninterrupted periods, he achieves more progress than days of fragmented work.

Mindfulness Techniques

Approach: Practise Mindfulness to Improve Attention

Let's meet Emily, a student juggling exams, part-time work and personal life:

Emily's Mindful Study Breaks: Emily practises mindfulness. Between study sessions, she meditates or practises deep breathing. These moments recharge her focus, allowing her to concentrate on one subject at a time.

Prioritization

Approach: Regularly Assess and Focus on High-Priority Tasks

Consider James, a startup founder managing product development, marketing, and investor relations:

James's Startup Compass: James evaluates tasks based on impact and deadlines. He tackles critical investor pitches before minor marketing tweaks. By prioritizing, he avoids spreading himself thin and ensures the startup's success.

The Dopamine Trap

Task switching provides a fleeting dopamine rush, creating a cycle of distraction and dependency. Media multitaskers often experience a thrill from switching tasks, but this high comes at a cost.

Juggling is an illusion, multitasking is a myth, and the true path to productivity and success lies in focused, single-task attention. By recognizing the costs of task switching and the benefits of dedicated focus, we can reclaim our time, enhance our effectiveness, and enrich our lives.

> *The key is not to prioritize what's on your schedule,*
> *but to schedule your priorities.*
>
> —Stephen Covey

Covey's wisdom highlights the necessity of focusing on what truly matters. By scheduling our most important tasks and giving them our full attention, we avoid the cognitive costs associated with task switching and ensure that our efforts are directed towards meaningful goals.

- **The "Neurosequential Tasking: Brain-Friendly Productivity" Concept:** Is it chaos or a symphony? Our brains thrive on rhythm. Imagine this: Each task, like a musical note, follows the next in a harmonious sequence. Neurosequential tasking aligns our activities with our brain's natural harmonies. Instead of juggling, we sequence tasks logically. Cognitive load decreases, focus sharpens. The outcome? A harmonious productivity where quality trumps quantity, akin to a maestro conducting a brain-friendly performance.

Movie Examples:

1. *Whiplash* **(2014)**—This film explores the intense relationship between a drummer and his instructor, highlighting how precise, sequential practice leads to mastery.
2. *The Social Network* **(2010)**—It depicts the creation of Facebook, emphasizing how focused, sequential development of ideas leads to groundbreaking success.
3. *Inception* **(2010)**—The meticulous planning and execution of the dream heist demonstrate the power of sequential tasking in achieving complex goals.

- **"The Attention Economy: Escaping the Dopamine Loop":** Our brains are wired for dopamine, drawn to novelty and instant rewards. Task switching fuels this addiction, creating a cycle of constant distraction. However, mindfulness and deep work offer a way out. By adopting these practices, we can escape the dopamine trap and achieve meaningful, lasting accomplishments.

Movie Examples:

1. ***The Social Dilemma* (2020)**—This documentary delves into the dark side of social media and the dopamine-driven attention economy, highlighting the need for mindful use.
2. ***Her* (2013)**—Explores the impact of technology on human relationships and the quest for deeper, more meaningful connections beyond instant gratification.
3. ***A Beautiful Mind* (2001)**—Follows the life of John Nash, whose focus on deep work leads to profound contributions to mathematics, despite his struggles with mental illness.

- **"Task Switching Tax: Paying the Cognitive Price":** Imagine each task switch as a toll on the cognitive highway. Whether moving from emails to reports or apps to brainstorming, there's a price to pay—not just in time but in cognitive resources. By understanding these costs, we can streamline our workflow, minimizing unnecessary detours and achieving better results.

Movie Examples:

1. ***Limitless* (2011)**—The protagonist's journey showcases the cognitive toll of rapid task switching and the benefits of sustained focus.
2. ***The Matrix* (1999)**—The movie illustrates the high cognitive load of switching between realities and the efficiency gained from mastering one environment.
3. ***Lucy* (2014)**—It explores the cognitive cost of accessing

vast amounts of information rapidly and the need for controlled, focused tasking to harness such power.
- **"Monotasking Renaissance: Quality Over Quantity"**: In a world enamoured with multitasking, monotasking reemerges as an art form. It celebrates doing one thing at a time with masterful focus. By prioritizing impact over volume, we can achieve higher quality results, reduce errors, enhance well-being, and find a balanced rhythm in our daily lives.

Movie Examples:

1. *Steve Jobs* **(2015)**—Focuses on the Apple co-founder's intense, monotasked drive to perfect his products, emphasizing quality over quantity.
2. *The Pursuit of Happyness* **(2006)**—Highlights the protagonist's single-minded focus on improving his life and achieving his goals despite numerous obstacles.
3. *Chef* **(2014)**—Demonstrates the joy and success found in focusing on one's passion with dedication, leading to high-quality outcomes in the culinary world.

- **"The Hidden Costs of Task Switching"**: Every time you switch tasks, you pay a cognitive toll. The initial decision to switch is quick, but the real cost lies in the time and effort required to reorient to the new task. For complex tasks, this switch can significantly increase the time needed to complete them. By understanding these hidden costs, we can better manage our tasks and improve overall productivity.

Movie Examples:

1. *The Devil Wears Prada* **(2006)**—This movie shows the protagonist's struggle with constant task switching in a high-pressure environment and the toll it takes on her.

2. ***Moneyball* (2011)**—It illustrates the cognitive toll of switching between traditional scouting methods and data-driven analysis, and the efficiency gained from focusing on one strategy.
3. ***Apollo 13* (1995)**—This highlights the critical importance of focused, sequential problem-solving in the face of life-threatening challenges, avoiding the costs of task switching.

So, what have we learnt?

Being busy does not always mean real work. The object of all work is production or accomplishment and to either of these ends there must be forethought, system, planning, intelligence and honest purpose, as well as perspiration.
Seeming to do is not doing.

—Thomas A. Edison

6

Killer Habits of the Superstars

*Our character is basically a composite of our habits.
Because they are consistent, often unconscious patterns,
they constantly, daily, express our character.*

—Stephen Covey

In our cultural narrative, the disciplined person often takes centre stage—a stoic figure who orchestrates life with unwavering control. But let's debunk this myth. We don't need more discipline; we need better navigation. Success isn't a marathon of rigid actions; it's a sprint fuelled by discipline long enough for habit to take the reins.

When tasks languish undone, we cry out for more discipline. But what we truly crave is habit—the silent architect of progress. Discipline trains us, moulds our actions, and eventually fades into a routine. Those "disciplined" individuals? They've mastered a handful of habits, not an ironclad will. No one is perpetually disciplined; it's neither feasible nor appealing.

Imagine every behaviour scripted by training—a robotic existence. It's both daunting and dull. Most people reach this crossroads: persist in the impossible or surrender quietly. Frustration knocks; resignation settles. But here's the secret:

success doesn't demand rigid discipline. It thrives on doing the right thing, not everything perfectly.

Success lies in choosing the right habit. Bring just enough discipline to lay its foundation. No Herculean effort is required. As this habit integrates into your life, you'll resemble a disciplined soul, but you won't be one. You'll be someone with a reliable ally—the habit you diligently nurtured. So embrace selective discipline, build your powerful habit, and let success unfold.

To illustrate this concept further, let's delve into the wisdom of some renowned minds who have touched upon the importance of discipline and habits in their unique ways:

Jocko Willink: Discipline Equals Freedom

Jocko Willink, a retired Navy SEAL and author, emphasizes that "discipline equals freedom." This might sound paradoxical at first, but it makes perfect sense when you think about it. The discipline to stick to your habits and routines ultimately frees you from the chaos of indecision and the burden of constant self-control. By ingraining positive habits, you create a structure within which you can operate freely and effectively.

Abraham Lincoln: The Choice of Priorities

Abraham Lincoln, one of the most revered US presidents, wisely said, "Discipline is choosing between what you want now and what you want most." This quote highlights the essence of delayed gratification, a critical component of habit formation. It's not about denying yourself pleasure; it's about prioritizing your long-term goals over short-term impulses. This disciplined choice, repeated consistently, transforms into a habit that drives you towards success.

David Campbell: The Memory of Desire

David Campbell succinctly put it: "Discipline is remembering what you want." This perspective shifts the focus from sheer willpower to a more intrinsic motivation. When you cultivate habits based on your deepest desires and goals, discipline becomes less of a struggle and more of a natural inclination. Your habits serve as constant reminders of your aspirations, steering you towards your objectives with less resistance.

James G. Bilkey: Pressure and Growth

James G. Bilkey emphasizes that without pressure, tension and discipline, we won't become our best selves. This idea ties into the concept of stress-induced growth. While excessive stress can be detrimental, a certain amount of pressure is necessary to push us out of our comfort zones and into the realm of growth and improvement. Habits formed under this constructive pressure can lead to significant personal development and achievement.

Dwight D. Eisenhower: Leadership and Discipline

Dwight D. Eisenhower, the thirty-fourth president of the United States and a five-star general during World War II, asserted that a commander who cannot develop proper discipline must be replaced. This statement underscores the importance of discipline in leadership. Effective leaders cultivate disciplined habits within themselves and their teams, creating an environment where success is not only possible but inevitable. By instilling good habits, leaders ensure that their teams operate efficiently and effectively, even under pressure.

Vince Lombardi: Faith and Discipline

Vince Lombardi, one of the most successful football coaches in history, pointed out that faith and discipline are essential even when you're not yet a winner. This perspective is crucial for understanding the journey to success. It's easy to be disciplined when you're already winning, but true discipline is maintaining your habits and faith in your process even when success seems distant. This unwavering commitment eventually leads to victory.

George Eliot: Genius and Discipline

George Eliot, a famous novelist, recognized that genius starts with a great capacity for receiving discipline. Her insight highlights the often-overlooked aspect of talent and genius: hard work and disciplined habits. Natural ability can only take you so far; it's the disciplined practice and the cultivation of productive habits that transform potential into true genius.

Jim Rohn: The Bridge Between Goals and Accomplishment

Jim Rohn, a renowned motivational speaker, wisely states, "Discipline is the bridge between goals and accomplishment." This quote encapsulates the entire argument: discipline is the means to an end, not the end itself. By establishing disciplined habits, you create a pathway to achieve your goals. Once these habits are in place, the need for constant discipline diminishes, as your habits carry you forward.

The myth of perpetual discipline is just that—a myth. True success lies in the mastery of habits. Discipline is necessary, but only to the extent that it helps you establish habits that align with your goals. Once these habits take root, they become the driving force behind your achievements. So, focus on cultivating the right habits, and let them guide you toward success.

Selected Discipline Spells Success

Take a look at Kavya Shivashankar, the 2009 Scripps National Spelling Bee Champion. As a young girl, she was intrigued by words and their meanings. Her father, himself a spelling bee aficionado, saw her interest and helped channel her curiosity into a structured study routine. Kavya wasn't merely disciplined in the general sense; she selected her focus with precision. Every day, she dedicated specific hours to studying word lists, understanding etymologies, and practising with mock spelling bees.

Kavya's journey wasn't about a strict, all-encompassing discipline but about a targeted one. She knew what needed her attention and gave it her all. This selected discipline paid off immensely. By consistently honing her skills in the right direction, she won not only the 2009 championship but also placed in the top 10 in previous years. Her focused effort turned into a habit of excellence in spelling, allowing her to achieve her dream.

The Power of Focused Effort

Similarly, Nihar Janga, the 2016 co-champion of the Scripps National Spelling Bee, exemplifies the power of focused effort. Nihar started his spelling journey at a very young age, guided by a clear and disciplined approach. He wasn't trying to master everything at once; instead, he focused on mastering one word at a time. This meticulous approach allowed him to build a strong foundation.

Nihar's daily routine included studying complex words, understanding their roots, and using them in sentences. His discipline was not about being rigorous in all areas of life but about channelling his efforts where they mattered the most. This selected discipline enabled him to become a spelling bee champion at just 11 years old, showcasing the extraordinary results of targeted focus and consistent practice.

Discipline in the Details

Consider the case of Ananya Vinay, the 2017 Scripps National Spelling Bee champion. Ananya's path to victory was paved with a disciplined yet flexible approach to learning. She embraced a routine that balanced rigorous study sessions with adequate rest and relaxation. Her discipline wasn't about grinding relentlessly but about smartly allocating her time and energy.

Ananya's training included breaking down complex words into manageable parts, studying their origins, and practising under pressure. Her ability to maintain discipline in her studies while also enjoying the process was crucial. This balanced, selected discipline helped her stay motivated and perform at her best, ultimately leading her to triumph in the national spotlight.

Liberation through Habit

The common thread among these spelling bee champions and Michael Phelps is their ability to harness selected discipline to form powerful habits. Their success stories highlight that discipline, when directed at the right habits, not only leads to exceptional achievements but also simplifies life. By focusing their efforts on what truly matters, they liberated themselves from the need to be disciplined in all areas.

In each of these cases, the disciplined efforts in their chosen fields—whether swimming or spelling—evolved into ingrained habits. These habits, in turn, drove their success and set them apart. The lesson is clear: by channelling your energy and discipline into forming the right habits, you can achieve great things while simplifying your life. So, find your sweet spot, focus your discipline where it counts, and let your habits guide you to success.

Mastering the Art of Habit Formation: A Comprehensive Journey

When we talk about habits, most people envision a daunting, nearly impossible task. The very idea of forming new habits can feel overwhelming. But fear not! The truth is, while habits may seem challenging at first, they become easier over time. It's all about the discipline and commitment you invest in the beginning. The reward? A life where the hard stuff becomes second nature.

The Role of Habits in Our Daily Lives

Research shows that about half of our daily actions are driven by repetition. This is why behavioural scientists and psychologists focus so much on establishing and maintaining positive habits. Regular sleep, exercise, a healthy diet, an organized schedule and mindfulness are just a few practices that can significantly improve our work, relationships and mental health. But how do you build these habits if they don't come naturally to you?

The Science of Habit Formation

Despite the abundance of hacks on the internet, the neuroscience behind habit formation doesn't offer shortcuts. Experts advocate for incremental progress. Dedicated commitment is the key to change. Interestingly, the first step toward creating long-term change involves building routines—not habits themselves.

Routines vs. Habits: Understanding the Difference

Many people think routines and habits are the same, but they aren't. James Clear, the author of *Atomic Habits*, explains that habits are behaviours done with little or no thought, while routines involve a series of behaviours frequently and intentionally repeated. Clear illustrates this distinction with the story of a reader who wanted to develop a habit of reading. Initially, she set up a routine of reading one page every night before bed, making it an intentional and repeated action. Over time, this routine transformed into a habit, where she would automatically pick up a book and start reading without even thinking about it. This demonstrates that for a behaviour to become a habit, it must first be a regularly performed routine.

The Challenge of Building Routines

Most people try to skip the "routine" phase, thinking habits will allow them to put tedious tasks on autopilot. This misconception often leads to disappointment. Unlike habits, routines are uncomfortable and require effort. For example, waking up early to run or meditating every night are initially hard to keep up. Habits, on the other hand, are so ingrained in our daily lives that it feels strange not to do them.

Transforming Routines into Habits

1. Define Your Objectives

Choose your behaviour thoughtfully and set realistic goals. Understand that developing new habits requires patience, self-discipline, and dedication. For example, a software developer might decide to spend 15 minutes each day learning a new programming language. This manageable start can lead to significant skill improvement over time.

2. Anticipate Challenges

Identify and address potential obstacles that have previously hindered you from maintaining this behaviour. For instance, a healthcare professional with a hectic schedule might struggle to find time for physical exercise. To overcome this, they could allocate 30 minutes on their daily schedule exclusively for a workout session. Additionally, finding a workout buddy can help maintain motivation and accountability.

3. Implement Small Changes

Take practical steps to initiate your new routine. Establish a consistent schedule for practising the behaviour. For example, a writer aiming to read more might set up Google Alerts for topics related to their field of interest. By dedicating specific times to read these alerts, they gradually build a habit of staying informed and inspired.

4. Pair Activities for Enjoyment

Combine a less enjoyable task with one you look forward to, making the process more appealing. For instance, an accountant might find it tedious to catch up on industry news. By pairing this task with listening to a favorite podcast or audiobook during a commute, the accountant can make the necessary activity more enjoyable and consistent.

The Myth of the 21-Day Habit Formation

The widely accepted notion that it takes 21 days to form a habit is overly simplistic. Research from 2009 provides a more nuanced understanding, revealing that habit formation timelines vary greatly. The study found that it can take anywhere from 18 to 254 days to establish a habit, with the average being around 66 days. The type of activity plays a crucial role in this process. For example, developing a habit of regular exercise might require several months, while establishing the habit of drinking more water each day could take only a few weeks. This variation underscores the importance of persistence and individualized approaches in habit formation.

Sustaining Momentum

Staying motivated can be challenging once the initial excitement wears off. Creating a specific plan and having accountability can help. Rewards are great motivators, especially when given immediately. For example, watch a movie while running on the treadmill instead of waiting until the end of the week.

Adaptive Persistence

It's normal to miss a day or two in any new routine. Instead of being rigid, be flexible and adjust your goals if needed. For instance, if running 10 miles daily is too hard, try jogging two miles three times a week. Gradually increase your effort as you get comfortable.

Self-Kindness Approach

Lastly, be compassionate with yourself. Long-term change takes time and there will be ups and downs. Use the tools and strategies you've learned to guide you when you feel off-track. Remember, as long as you keep at an activity, you will get better at it—no matter how long it takes.

In conclusion, mastering the art of habit formation is a journey. It requires discipline, commitment and patience. But with the right approach, you can turn challenging routines into effortless habits and achieve lasting change. So, start today and transform your life one habit at a time.

7

Mindfulness: The True Power of Positivity

*The present moment is filled with joy and happiness.
If you are attentive, you will see it.*

—Thich Nhat Hanh

Cultivating Mindfulness Instead of Relying Solely on Willpower

Why intentionally choose the arduous path? Why willingly place yourself in challenging situations or work with unnecessary constraints? Most people unknowingly do so every day. When we link our success exclusively to willpower without acknowledging its limitations, we set ourselves up for disappointment. But it doesn't have to be this way.

"In life's intricate dance, willpower and timing waltz together, shaping our path to achievement."

Recognizing this interplay allows us to move gracefully toward our goals.

The dance between willpower and timing is a delicate balancing act where willpower, defined as our ability to exert self-control, resist temptations, and make deliberate choices, functions like a muscle that can be strengthened through practise, helping us stay focused, overcome obstacles, and pursue our goals for long-term success. However, willpower isn't always readily available as it fluctuates based on fatigue, stress and external distractions. On the other hand, timing involves recognizing when to act, understanding that sometimes waiting for the right moment is wiser than pushing forward impulsively, and capitalizing on flow states where we're fully immersed in an activity, aligning with our natural rhythms to enhance productivity. Life often presents opportunities at unexpected times, and recognizing and seizing these moments can lead to breakthroughs. Balancing willpower and timing requires finesse; pushing too hard without considering timing can exhaust us, while waiting too long can result in missed opportunities. Listening to our intuition, which often knows when to act, and being adaptable to adjust our pace or change direction mid-dance, ensures we move harmoniously through life's challenges and opportunities.

At first, it seemed simple: Summon our will, and success would naturally follow. We set out on this path. Unfortunately, it turned out to be a short-lived journey. As we tried to impose our will on our defenseless goals, we faced a discouraging reality: willpower wasn't always within our grasp. One moment it was there, and the next—it disappeared. It ebbed and flowed, almost as if it had its own agenda. Building success solely on the back of on-demand willpower was fruitless. We started to question ourselves: Were we flawed? Failures? Maybe. We thought we lacked determination, inner strength, and resilience. So, we doubled our efforts and came to a humbling conclusion: Willpower isn't always at our beck and call.

Despite our motivation, willpower didn't always enforce our wishes. Our belief—that it would always be available—was mistaken. Willpower isn't an ever-present resource.

Throughout much of our lives, we barely considered willpower. Then, it caught our attention. The capacity to control ourselves and influence our actions is incredibly powerful. When anchored in discipline, it transforms into an unstoppable force. However, relying solely on willpower because we think we can—well, that's pure, unrefined power. The essence of willpower.

Most people recognize willpower's importance but underestimate its true significance. An unconventional research project unveiled its depths.

Embracing Mindfulness

Rather than relying solely on willpower, mindfulness offers a sustainable path. Mindfulness entails complete presence in the moment, observing thoughts and feelings without judgement. This awareness allows us to recognize waning willpower and make conscious choices.

Through mindfulness, we gain insight into our motivations and better manage our actions. Rather than battling innate impulses, we learn to collaborate with them, achieving a harmonious balance between effort and ease. This equilibrium fosters consistent, enduring success.

The Strength of Being Present

Mindfulness isn't about suppressing desires or coercion. It's about intentional engagement with experiences. When mindful, we navigate challenges with clarity and resilience, even when willpower wavers.

Mindfulness teaches us to:

1. **Acknowledge Limits**: Recognize that willpower has bounds, enabling realistic goal-setting.

2. **Practise Self-Compassion**: Replace harsh self-criticism with understanding and appreciation for our efforts.
3. **Make Deliberate Choices**: Stay present, align decisions with values and long-term aspirations.

In this dance between mindfulness and willpower, we discover a more profound source of strength—one that transcends mere determination.

Explore this path of mindfulness, where presence becomes your compass toward lasting happiness.

Let's talk about two experiments. In the vibrant era of the late 1960s and early 1970s, Walter Mischel, a pioneering psychologist, embarked on a groundbreaking journey at Stanford University's Bing Nursery School. His mission was to delve into the intricacies of willpower among young children, a quest that would soon become legendary as "The Marshmallow Test." This experiment, which involved more than 500 eager and curious four-year-olds, sought to understand how early self-control could shape future success.

The 1920 Little Albert Experiment by John B. Watson and his graduate student Rosalie Rayner was notable in psychology. The experiment examined human classical conditioning. In this study, "Little Albert," a nine-month-old baby, was exposed to a white rat, rabbit, monkey, masks and burning newspapers. Albert initially didn't mind these stimulations. Watson and Rayner would combine the white rat with a loud, frightening noise (hammering a steel bar) to scare Albert. After repeated pairings, Albert associated the white rat with the loud noise and showed fear responses to the rodent alone, proving that humans can learn fear.

Comparative Study: Marshmallow Test vs. Little Albert Experiment in Determining Human Mindfulness

Mindfulness, as a practice, emphasizes being present and fully engaged with the current moment. This state of active, open attention to the present can be influenced by various psychological traits and behaviours. Two landmark studies—the Marshmallow Test and the Little Albert Experiment—provide valuable insights into aspects of human behaviour related to mindfulness. This comparative study explores how these experiments inform our understanding of mindfulness, willpower, and the emotional responses that shape our actions.

The Marshmallow Test

Overview

Conducted by Walter Mischel in the late 1960s and early 1970s, the Marshmallow Test measured young children's ability to delay gratification. The test involved offering a child a choice: eat one marshmallow immediately or wait 15 minutes and receive two marshmallows. The child's decision reflected their ability to exercise self-control, an aspect closely linked to mindfulness.

Methodology

- **Participants**: Preschool children aged 4–6 years.
- **Procedure**: Each child was left alone in a room with a marshmallow and given the option to eat it immediately or wait to receive a second marshmallow.
- **Observation**: Researchers observed the children's behaviour and strategies to resist the temptation.

Findings

- **Delayed Gratification**: Children who waited demonstrated higher levels of self-control.
- **Long-Term Correlations**: Follow-up studies showed that children who delayed gratification tended to have better academic performance, social skills, and stress management in later life.

The Little Albert Experiment

Overview

The Little Albert Experiment, conducted by John B. Watson and Rosalie Rayner in 1920, aimed to demonstrate classical conditioning in humans. By associating a neutral stimulus (a white rat) with a loud noise, they conditioned a child to fear the rat, illustrating how emotional responses can be conditioned.

Methodology

- **Participants**: A nine-month-old infant named "Albert."
- **Procedure**: Albert was initially shown a white rat without any fear. Watson and Rayner then paired the sight of the rat with a loud noise. After several pairings, Albert exhibited fear at the sight of the rat alone.
- **Generalization**: Albert's fear extended to other furry objects, such as rabbits and dogs.

Findings

- **Classical Conditioning**: It demonstrated that emotional responses could be conditioned in humans.
- **Ethical Concerns**: The experiment raised significant ethical issues due to the distress caused to Albert and the lack of desensitization afterward.

Insights on Mindfulness from the Experiments

The Marshmallow Test: Willpower and Mindfulness

- **Willpower as a Finite Resource**: The Marshmallow Test illustrates that willpower can be depleted. Children who managed to delay gratification employed strategies that align with mindfulness practices, such as distraction and focusing on future rewards.
- **Mindfulness in Action**: The children's ability to stay present and resist immediate gratification is a form of mindfulness. It shows the importance of self-awareness and self-regulation in achieving long-term goals.

The Little Albert Experiment: Emotional Responses and Mindfulness

- **Conditioned Emotional Responses**: The Little Albert Experiment demonstrates how conditioned emotional responses can disrupt mindfulness. Albert's learned fear response shows how negative experiences can create automatic, unconscious reactions that hinder present-moment awareness.
- **Implications for Mindfulness Practice**: Understanding how fears and conditioned responses develop can help in cultivating mindfulness. Mindfulness practices can aid in recognizing and managing these conditioned responses, promoting emotional regulation and reducing unconscious reactivity.

Mindfulness: The True Power of Positivity

The Dance between Willpower and Timing

- **Willpower as a Muscle**: Willpower functions like a muscle that can be strengthened through practise but can also become fatigued. Effective use of willpower involves

recognizing its limits and replenishing it through rest and positive emotions.
- **Timing and Flow**: Aligning actions with natural rhythms and recognizing the right moments to act are crucial. This interplay ensures that willpower is used efficiently, avoiding burnout and maximizing productivity.

Embracing Mindfulness

- **Awareness and Presence**: Mindfulness involves being fully present and aware of one's thoughts and feelings. This state helps in recognizing when willpower is waning and allows for more conscious decision-making.
- **Self-Compassion**: Mindfulness encourages self-compassion, which reduces harsh self-criticism and fosters a supportive inner dialogue. This approach enhances resilience and sustained effort toward goals.

Integrating Positive Emotions

- **Gratitude**: Enhances self-control and perseverance. Keeping a gratitude journal can maintain this positive emotion.
- **Empathy**: Fosters caring for others and oneself, reducing impulsive reactions.
- **Authentic Pride**: Motivates tackling challenging tasks and making beneficial decisions. Encouraging a growth mindset supports this positive emotion.

Both the Marshmallow Test and the Little Albert Experiment offer valuable insights into the interplay between mindfulness, willpower, and emotional responses. The Marshmallow Test highlights the importance of self-control and delayed gratification, key aspects of mindfulness. The Little Albert Experiment accentuates the impact of conditioned emotional responses on behaviour, illustrating the need for mindfulness practices to manage and mitigate these automatic reactions. By integrating mindfulness with an understanding of willpower's limitations and the power of positive emotions, individuals can cultivate a sustainable path to success and well-being.

Moreover, the concept of "ego depletion" introduced by Roy Baumeister and his colleagues added another layer of complexity to our understanding of willpower. Their research suggested that self-control is like a muscle that can become fatigued with use. In one experiment, participants who were asked to resist eating freshly baked cookies subsequently performed worse on tasks requiring self-control compared to those who had not exerted such restraint. This supported the idea that willpower is limited and can be drained, impacting behaviour and decision-making.

Additionally, the dual-self model proposed by Richard Thaler and Hersh Shefrin offered an economic perspective on self-control. According to this model, human behaviour is influenced by two conflicting "selves": a "doer" focused on immediate gratification and a "planner" concerned with long-term goals. The tension between these selves can lead to time-inconsistent preferences, where individuals make decisions that favor short-term desires over long-term benefits. Understanding this internal conflict has important implications for designing interventions that promote better self-control.

The field of neuroscience has also contributed to our understanding of willpower. Studies using functional magnetic resonance imaging (fMRI) have shown that self-control involves the prefrontal cortex, which is responsible for executive functions such as planning and decision-making. Research by Antonio Rangel and his colleagues revealed that the ability to delay gratification is associated with increased activity in the prefrontal cortex, highlighting the brain's role in regulating self-control.

Understanding the distinction between impulsive and reflective systems in the brain has also enriched the concept of self-control. The dual-systems theory, which posits that self-control involves the interaction between an impulsive system driven by immediate rewards and a reflective system focused on long-term goals, has provided a framework for understanding the neural and cognitive mechanisms underlying self-control. This theory suggests that enhancing the reflective system's influence can promote better decision-making and self-regulation.

Moreover, the idea of automatic self-control, where self-control processes are triggered without conscious effort, has gained traction. This perspective challenges the traditional view that self-control is always a deliberate, effortful process. Instead, it suggests that certain self-control strategies can become automatized through practise and conditioning, enabling individuals to resist temptations more effectively without expending significant cognitive resources.

In conclusion, the exploration of willpower through Mischel's Marshmallow Test and subsequent research has revealed that self-control is a critical factor in shaping our lives. Early deferral of gratification predicts future success, affecting everything from academic achievement to health and financial stability. However, willpower is not an unlimited resource and can be depleted, making it essential to manage and harness it effectively. As we continue to uncover the complexities of self-control, it becomes increasingly clear that fostering willpower in children and adults alike is a vital investment in their long-term well-being and success.

The Emotional Powerhouse

Imagine your willpower as a power bar on your cell phone. Each morning you wake up with a fully charged battery, but as the day progresses and you face temptations, the charge depletes. When your battery hits red, your ability to resist temptations falters. Willpower is a finite resource that can be replenished with downtime, but it's not infinite. This is where positive emotions come into play—they act like a renewable energy source for your willpower.

Thankfulness

Thankfulness is like a quick boost for your willpower. When you feel thankful, it's as if your battery gets an extra charge. In a study mimicking the famous Marshmallow Test, participants who were asked to recall a time they felt grateful showed almost double the self-control compared to those who felt happy or neutral. Gratitude not only enhances self-control but also promotes perseverance in various contexts, such as helping others or making prudent health choices. Keeping a gratitude journal and reflecting on small, frequent moments of gratitude can help maintain this positive emotion, thereby boosting your willpower.

Empathy

Empathy is another powerful emotion that can recharge your willpower. It extends beyond gratitude, focusing on caring for others and even your future self. In a study, participants who saw older versions of themselves saved twice as much for retirement as those who saw their current selves. Compassion reduces impulsive reactions and promotes wise decision-making. Engaging in activities that foster compassion, like meditation or synchronizing with others through group activities, can enhance your willpower by keeping your emotions in a positive state.

Self-Importance

Self-awareness and self-importance, when authentic and not hubristic, can also power your willpower battery. It stems from accomplishing goals and being recognized for your abilities, reinforcing your self-control and perseverance. People who experience pride are more motivated to tackle challenging tasks and make long-term beneficial decisions. Encouraging a growth mindset and recognizing efforts over mere success can foster authentic pride, thereby supporting your willpower.

Win at Life Without Losing Your Mind

Positive emotions like gratitude, compassion, and pride not only boost willpower but also enhance social relationships, leading to greater happiness and success. Instead of solely relying on willpower, cultivating these emotions can create a sustainable and renewable source of energy for achieving your goals. So, embrace these positive emotions, and you'll find a lasting boost to your willpower and overall well-being.

Kickstart Ninja Thoughts

Alright, martial arts enthusiasts, tighten those belts and get ready to kick through the world of exercise motivation with a side of humour and a roundhouse kick of laughter. Staying fit isn't just about avoiding the couch or resisting the allure of skipping the dojo. It's about syncing your actions with your fitness goals and finding the motivation to keep going. Let's explore this with a hilarious martial arts twist.

Imagine your body is a high-performance martial arts machine. Yep, that's right. This complex system needs the right fuel to operate at peak efficiency. Your brain, a small part of your body mass, burns through a whopping one-fifth of your calories. If it were a car, it'd be the kind that makes you cringe at the gas station. Most of our conscious activity buzzes around in the prefrontal cortex—the dojo's control center, handling focus, short-term memory, problem-solving and impulse control. It's essentially the headquarters of our training motivation.

Last In, First Out: The Martial Arts Version of Sparring

Here's where it gets interesting. The brain operates on a "last in, first out" basis. The newest parts of our brain, like the prefrontal cortex, are the first to suffer when there's a resource shortage. So, when you skip a meal before training, your basic survival functions (like breathing) get first dibs on the energy, and your exercise motivation gets left in the dust, whining like a rookie during a tough sparring session.

Motivation: A Delicate Balance

Think of exercise motivation like a delicate balance—it needs constant attention. A 2007 study revealed that our motivation takes a hit when our blood sugar levels drop. Researchers found that participants who performed physically demanding tasks showed a significant decrease in glucose levels. They also discovered that those who consumed real sugar performed better on subsequent tasks compared to those who had a sugar substitute. So, next time you need to power through a tough training session, think of it as refuelling your motivation engine with the right kind of energy—preferably not the kind that makes you crash into a sugar coma later.

Aligning Actions with Goals: The Martial Arts Secret

Here's the kicker: Exercise motivation isn't just about pushing through tough training; it's about aligning your actions with your core fitness goals. When you're genuinely motivated and your actions reflect your deepest desires, you experience less motivation depletion. It's like having a secret stash of energy drinks for your martial arts routine. Intrinsic motivation is the name of the game.

The Martial Arts Challenge: A Lesson in Patience

Remember the Marshmallow Test? Picture a bunch of four-year-olds trying not to eat a marshmallow for 15 minutes. Hilarious, right? Well, it turns out those who resisted the marshmallow had better life outcomes—higher SAT scores, better stress management and lower rates of drug addiction. It's all about delayed gratification and using motivation wisely, much like mastering a challenging martial arts technique.

The Comedy of Motivation Depletion

Just like a comedian running out of jokes, our exercise motivation runs out too. Stanford researchers found that students asked to remember a seven-digit number were twice as likely to choose chocolate cake over fruit salad compared to those remembering a two-digit number. That extra cognitive load zapped their motivation. So, managing motivation is all about timing and knowing when to use it, just like timing your strikes in a sparring match.

Fuel for Fitness: Eat Your Way to Mastery

Finally, let's talk about food. Your brain is a high-maintenance organ that demands the best fuel. Complex carbs and proteins are like premium gasoline for your brain, keeping your motivation engine running smoothly. So, the next time you're about to tackle a challenging training session, make sure you've got the right snacks on hand.

Exercise motivation isn't just about brute strength; it's about smart management. Align your actions with your goals, keep your brain well-fed, and remember that timing is everything. And when in doubt, laugh it off—after all, humour is the best motivator. Now, get out there and kick some motivation into your martial arts training!

Martial Arts Mastery: The Power of Willpower

One of the real challenges in martial arts and life is that when our willpower is low, we tend to fall back on our default settings. Researchers Angela Duckworth from the University of Pennsylvania, along with Roy Baumeister from Florida State University and Kathleen Vohs from the University of Minnesota, found a creative way to investigate this. They analysed the impact of willpower on decision-making in high-stress environments.

Study Design and Methodology

The study involved a meticulous analysis of various high-stress environments, including corporate boardrooms, emergency response units and competitive sports settings. The researchers used a mixed-method approach, combining quantitative data collection with qualitative interviews to capture a holistic view of willpower dynamics.

For the quantitative part, the researchers collected data from over 2,000 participants across different sectors. They monitored decision-making patterns, performance metrics and physiological indicators of stress, such as cortisol levels and heart rate variability. Participants were subjected to a series of tasks designed to simulate high-stress scenarios, such as making quick, high-stakes decisions under time pressure. In addition to quantitative measures, the researchers conducted in-depth interviews with 150 participants, including executives, emergency responders, and professional athletes. These interviews aimed to gather personal experiences and perceptions regarding how individuals felt their willpower influenced their decision-making and performance.

Key Findings: Willpower Depletion and Default Settings

The study confirmed that **when willpower is low, individuals tend to fall back on their default settings or habitual behaviours.** This phenomenon was consistently observed across all high-stress environments. Participants reported that during periods of fatigue or mental exhaustion, they were more likely to revert to routine actions, even if those actions were suboptimal.

One of the most striking findings was the impact of willpower depletion on decision-making quality. **In the initial stages of high-stress tasks, participants made more rational and well-considered decisions. However, as their willpower waned, the quality of their decisions deteriorated significantly.** For instance, executives who started the day with strategic, long-term planning sessions often resorted to more conservative, risk-averse choices by the afternoon, when their mental resources were depleted.

Physiological Impact

The physiological data revealed that **willpower depletion was closely linked to increased cortisol levels and reduced heart rate variability, both indicators of stress.** This finding suggested that the body's stress response plays a crucial role in diminishing willpower. Participants with higher baseline stress levels showed quicker depletion of willpower and were more prone to making impulsive decisions.

Sector-Specific Observations

- **Corporate Environment:** In corporate settings, decision fatigue led to a higher reliance on established protocols and a reluctance to innovate. Executives were less likely to endorse creative solutions later in the day.
- **Emergency Response:** For emergency responders, the stakes were particularly high. The study found that decision fatigue could lead to critical errors in judgement, such as delayed responses or misallocation of resources. This highlighted the importance of structured breaks and support systems to maintain optimal performance.
- **Competitive Sports:** Athletes demonstrated a clear pattern of performance decline corresponding with willpower depletion. **Those who managed their energy levels effectively, through techniques like mindfulness and proper nutrition, maintained higher performance consistency.**

Implications for Practice

The study's findings have profound implications for various fields:

1. **Strategic Planning:** Organizations can optimize decision-making processes by scheduling critical tasks during periods of peak willpower. This might involve restructuring the workday to include more breaks and mental rest periods.
2. **Training Programmes:** Incorporating willpower management strategies into training programmes can help individuals better cope with high-stress situations.

Techniques such as mindfulness, adequate nutrition and physical exercise were found to bolster willpower reserves.
3. **Policy Development:** In high-stakes fields like emergency response, developing policies that mandate regular breaks and provide psychological support can mitigate the adverse effects of willpower depletion.

Harnessing the Power of Willpower

Our willpower often falters not because we are conscious of it, but because we overlook it entirely. Without recognizing that willpower fluctuates, we allow it to ebb away unnoticed. This lack of mindfulness can transform our determination from strong and resolute to weak and wavering, hindering our path to success.

Consider willpower as a spectrum of strength. Like a battery indicator that shifts from green to red, there exists both "willpower" and "won't power." Many people inadvertently bring "won't power" to their most critical challenges, making them even more daunting. When we fail to see willpower as a finite resource that needs to be conserved, focused on essential tasks, and replenished regularly, we set ourselves up for a difficult journey towards our goals.

So, how can you effectively harness your willpower? **You must acknowledge its presence, monitor its levels, and treat it with respect. Prioritize tasks that matter the most during times when your willpower is at its peak.** In essence, ensure you allocate your peak willpower periods to the most significant aspects of your life. This conscious effort to manage and utilize willpower effectively is crucial for achieving sustained success.

Your Willpower Red alerts!

Ninja Panic Mode:

- Handling Fear: Coping with fear and anxiety uses up a lot of your willpower. It's like facing a horde of ninjas with a toothpick!

Pizza Perils:

- Resisting Temptations: Saying no to temptations takes a toll on your self-control. Think of it as avoiding the last slice of pizza while on a diet.

Karate Chop Restraint:

- Inhibiting Impulses: Suppressing spontaneous actions demands a high level of self-control. Imagine not throwing a karate chop when someone cuts you in line.

Kale Smoothie Struggle:

- Adopting New Habits: Initiating and sticking to new behaviours can be mentally taxing. It's like trying to switch from burgers to kale smoothies.

Impress-a-thon Fatigue:

- Seeking Approval: Trying to impress others can be mentally exhausting. Think of it as performing your best kata in front of a crowd that includes your childhood rival.

Training vs. Binge-Watching Battle:

- Choosing Long-Term Goals: Opting for long-term benefits over immediate rewards requires sustained willpower. It's like choosing to train every day rather than binge-watching your favorite martial arts movies.

Dojo Cleaning Duty:

- Engaging in Unpleasant Tasks: Doing things you don't enjoy is a significant drain on your mental resources. Imagine cleaning the dojo toilets after a chili cook-off.

Headband Heist Calm:

- Suppressing Emotions: Keeping your emotions in check can deplete your willpower reserves. Picture yourself staying calm when your opponent steals your lucky headband.

Grandmaster Exam Gauntlet:

- Taking Examinations: The mental strain of taking tests can quickly drain your willpower. It's like sparring with a grandmaster while reciting a poem.

Meditation Mayhem:

- Managing Distractions: Constantly filtering out distractions requires significant mental effort. It's like trying to meditate while your sensei is playing the drums.

Aggression Zen Master:

- Controlling Aggression: Restraining aggressive impulses requires considerable mental energy. Picture a black belt holding back when a white belt critiques their form.

Imagine you're running a marathon with a leaky water bottle. With every step, you lose more of your precious hydration, and soon you're unable to finish the race strong. This is how it feels when your motivation and positivity drain away through unnoticed daily activities. Managing these crucial resources is essential.

The timing of when you harness your motivation and positivity is critical. To tackle your most important tasks effectively, you need these resources at their peak. If you start your day by focusing on your key priorities—your ONE GOAL—while your motivation and positivity are still high, you set yourself up for success.

Throughout the day, as your self-control wanes, having enough motivation and positivity left helps prevent distractions and keeps you on track. Using your energy wisely ensures that you don't undo your hard work.

By prioritizing early in the day, you make the most of your strongest moments. Motivation and positivity, much like any set resource, must be carefully managed to maintain focus and achieve your goals.

Golden Nuggets:

Managing Your Emotional and Mental Reserves

1. **Don't scatter your motivation.** Every day, you only have so much motivation to go around. Prioritize what's important and focus your motivation on those key tasks.
2. **Keep an eye on your positivity levels.** Staying positive takes energy, so make sure you're fuelling your body and mind with the right nourishment. Regular meals and healthy eating are essential.

8

The Palace of Stable Dreams

The key to keeping your balance is knowing when you've lost it.

—Anonymous

"Balance is a mythical unicorn we chase but never catch." The concept of balancing work and life is not just unrealistic; it is fundamentally flawed and can lead to more harm than good. The quest for balance often leaves us feeling perpetually off-kilter, as the very nature of life is dynamic and ever-changing. Instead of striving for balance, we should seek **purpose, meaning and significance**, which inevitably involves embracing the imbalance that comes with pursuing what truly matters.

The Illusion of Perfect Equilibrium

Stability is often viewed as a static state, a serene equilibrium where everything gets equal attention. **This is a fallacy.** Stability, in reality, is a constant act of balancing. Like a tightrope walker adjusting their weight to stay on the line, life requires continuous adjustments. The idea of a "balanced life" is a **seductive but dangerous myth**. It suggests that a perfectly equal distribution of time and energy across all aspects of life is not only possible but desirable.

The Historical Context

Historically, the concept of balance is a modern luxury. **For most of human history, work was life.** Survival depended on hunting, farming and other labour-intensive activities. With the advent of agricultural surplus, professional specialization emerged, allowing some people to focus on trades or intellectual pursuits while others produced food. The Industrial Revolution further complicated this, introducing the notion of fixed work hours and the separation of work from personal life. The term "work–life balance" only entered common parlance in the mid-1980s, reflecting societal shifts as more women joined the workforce.

The Modern Dilemma

In the contemporary socio-technological landscape, the pervasive influence of technology has profoundly exacerbated the sense of imbalance experienced by individuals. The omnipresence of digital connectivity blurs the demarcations between professional responsibilities and personal life, fostering an illusion that one must perpetually juggle all aspects of existence simultaneously. This phenomenon, often termed as the "always-on" culture, demands a nuanced philosophical and sociological understanding to fully grasp its implications on human life.

The Philosophical Underpinnings

From a philosophical standpoint, the relentless integration of technology into daily life challenges the Aristotelian concept of *eudaimonia*, or human flourishing. Aristotle posited that a balanced life, one that harmonizes work, leisure and contemplation, is essential for achieving true well-being. In stark contrast, the modern technological paradigm undermines this balance by fostering a continuous state of activity and engagement. This disruption can be seen as a deviation from the classical ideals of balance and moderation, leading to a state of perpetual dissatisfaction and existential anxiety.

Sociological Dimensions

Sociologically, the intrusion of technology into the private sphere can be analysed through the lens of Habermas's theory of the public sphere. The conflation of work and personal life erodes the distinction between the public and private realms, resulting in a phenomenon where the boundaries of personal time and space are incessantly encroached upon by professional demands. This shift reflects a broader societal trend towards the commodification of time, where every moment is viewed as a potential opportunity for productivity.

The sociological impact of this technological encroachment is particularly pronounced among women, who often bear a disproportionate burden of balancing professional and domestic responsibilities. The phenomenon of the "second shift," as described by sociologist Arlie Hochschild, highlights how working women undertake a "second shift" of unpaid domestic labour after completing their professional workday. This dual burden is intensified by the constant connectivity enabled by technology, leading to heightened stress and burnout.

Women Navigating the Modern Dilemma

1. **Sheryl Sandberg**: The ex-COO of Facebook, Meta Platforms, Sheryl Sandberg, has openly discussed her challenges in balancing a high-powered career with her responsibilities as a mother. Sandberg's advocacy for workplace policies that support work–life balance, such as flexible hours and parental leave, underscores the necessity of structural changes to mitigate the pressures faced by working women in the technology-driven era.
2. **Jacinda Ardern**: The former prime minister of New Zealand, Jacinda Ardern, became a global symbol of work–life balance when she gave birth while in office. Ardern's experience illustrates the complexities of managing leadership roles alongside personal life, and her approach has sparked conversations about the need for societal and institutional support for working mothers.
3. **Serena Williams**: As a professional athlete and a mother, Serena Williams has navigated the challenges of maintaining peak performance in her career while fulfilling her role as a parent. Williams's candid discussions about her struggles with postpartum depression and work–life balance highlight the intersection of mental health and the demands of modern professional life.

Terms such as "role conflict," "time famine," and "boundary management" are central to understanding the dynamics at play. Role conflict refers to the tension arising from competing demands of different roles, while time famine describes the pervasive feeling of having insufficient time to fulfill all responsibilities. Boundary management encompasses strategies employed by individuals to negotiate the interface between work and personal life, aiming to create distinct boundaries to preserve well-being.

The modern dilemma of work–life balance, exacerbated by technology, necessitates a multidisciplinary approach that integrates philosophical insights and sociological analysis. By examining real-life examples of women who navigate these challenges, we gain a deeper understanding of the structural and individual factors that contribute to this pervasive issue. Addressing this dilemma requires both personal strategies for boundary management and systemic changes to support a more balanced and fulfilling life for all individuals.

The Theory of Dreams

In our pursuit of a balanced life, we often overlook the profound influence of our dreams. Dreams are not just the whimsical wanderings of our minds during sleep; they are reflections of our deepest desires and fears. **Dreams provide insight into our subconscious**, highlighting the areas of our lives that crave attention and fulfillment. By paying attention to our dreams, we can identify what truly matters to us, allowing us to prioritize our waking hours accordingly.

The Decision Fatigue Theory

Another critical aspect to consider is the Decision Fatigue Theory. **This theory suggests that making many decisions throughout the day depletes willpower, leading to decision fatigue.** As individuals make more decisions, their ability to exert self-control diminishes, resulting in poorer choices later in the day. Strategies to combat decision fatigue include simplifying choices, creating routines, and making important decisions early in the day. This approach not only conserves mental energy but also ensures that our most crucial decisions are made when our minds are freshest.

The Dangers of Middle Mismanagement

Striving for balance often means settling for the middle, where everything gets some attention but nothing gets enough. This mediocrity prevents us from achieving **extraordinary results**. True success and fulfillment come from focusing intensely on what matters most, even if it means letting other things slide temporarily. The magic happens at the extremes, not in the middle.

Real-Life Lessons on Time

Time waits for no one, and postponing important aspects of life for future fulfillment can lead to regret. A poignant example is the story of a schoolteacher and a farmer who saved diligently for retirement, only to have their plans thwarted by illness and death. This narrative underscores the **impermanence of life** and the folly of delaying joy and connection for a future that may never come.

Stable Dreams and Counterbalancing

The concept of stable dreams integrates the essence of dreams reflecting waking life with the dynamic equilibrium required in our daily existence. Stable dreams propose that our subconscious mind, through dreams, perpetually strives to balance the multifaceted aspects of our waking lives. This balance, or counterbalance, is crucial for mental well-being, providing insights into how we manage and prioritize our waking activities and emotions. Drawing from the study of work–life balance in dreams, we can extend this theory to better understand the interplay between our conscious and subconscious experiences.

The Essence of Counterbalancing

Counterbalancing transcends the mere notion of achieving balance; it encompasses making significant, purposeful time commitments to what matters most, while ensuring other life aspects are periodically addressed. This dynamic adjustment is akin to a ballerina's constant, minute corrections that maintain her poised and graceful stance. Counterbalancing thus becomes a fluid process, continually readjusting to sustain equilibrium in the face of life's varying demands.

The Theory of Stable Dreams

To deepen our understanding of stable dreams and the concept of counterbalancing, we can turn to the insights of two contemporary philosophers of dream studies: Dr Deirdre Barrett and Dr Mark Blagrove. Their extensive work on the psychology of dreams provides a profound foundation to expand the theory of stable dreams.

Dr Deirdre Barrett, renowned for her work on dreams and their impact on creativity and problem-solving, argues that dreams serve as a unique form of cognitive processing. In her 2001 book *The Committee of Sleep,* Barrett posits that dreams can facilitate innovative solutions and emotional processing by allowing the mind to explore and integrate waking life experiences in a safe, imaginative space. This perspective supports the idea that dreams are not random but purposeful, reflecting our efforts to maintain a dynamic balance in our waking lives.

Dr Mark Blagrove, a leading researcher on the social and emotional functions of dreaming, emphasizes the role of dreams in emotional regulation and social cognition. Blagrove's research suggests that dreams help process and regulate emotions, contributing to psychological resilience. This aligns with the theory of stable dreams, where the subconscious mind uses dreams to mirror and address waking life imbalances, thereby fostering mental well-being.

The Concept of Counterbalancing

Drawing from the works of Barrett and Blagrove, the concept of counterbalancing becomes even more profound. Rather than seeking a static state of balance, we should aim for counterbalancing. This means making significant time commitments to what matters most while ensuring we periodically address other areas of our lives. Counterbalancing involves a dynamic adjustment, much like a ballerina making minute corrections to appear poised and graceful.

Barrett's insights into the cognitive functions of dreams suggest that when we engage deeply in our primary tasks, our dreams help us process these experiences, leading to innovative ideas and emotional resolution. Similarly, Blagrove's emphasis on emotional regulation through dreams underscores the importance of periodically shifting focus to personal needs to maintain emotional health.

Types of Counterbalancing

1. Between Work and Personal Life

This requires giving disproportionate time to your most important work tasks while ensuring that personal needs are not neglected for too long. Barrett's theory supports this by highlighting that dreams can help integrate intense work experiences, fostering creative problem-solving and emotional clarity. However, Blagrove's research warns that neglecting personal needs for too long can disrupt emotional regulation, leading to increased stress and diminished well-being.

2. Within Work and Personal Life

Recognizing that different aspects of life need varying levels of attention at different times is crucial. For example, during a major work project, you might focus intensely on work, but afterwards, you must return to personal commitments. Barrett's idea of the cognitive processing function of dreams suggests that during intense work periods, dreams might help consolidate work-related learning and innovation. Blagrove's emphasis on emotional regulation implies that post project, shifting attention to personal life can help restore emotional balance and resilience.

The Palace of Stable Dreams

Imagine a vast, intricate palace where each room represents a different aspect of your life—work, family, hobbies, health and personal growth. This palace is the embodiment of your stable dreams, each room meticulously maintained and decorated, reflecting the dynamic adjustments you make in your waking life.

In the Palace of Stable Dreams, Dr Barrett's and Dr Blagrove's theories come to life. Each night, as you navigate the palace in your dreams, you explore different rooms based on your waking life priorities and stresses. When work demands your focus, you find yourself in the grand hall of professional achievements, where your mind creatively processes work-related challenges and innovations. As personal needs arise, you drift into the serene garden of personal life, where emotional regulation and social connections flourish.

This palace is a testament to the dynamic, ongoing process of counterbalancing. It showcases the seamless integration of waking life experiences and dreams, emphasizing that maintaining mental well-being requires a fluid, adaptable approach to life's ever-changing demands. By embracing the concept of stable dreams and counterbalancing, you ensure that each room in your palace remains vibrant and harmonious, reflecting a well-balanced, fulfilling life.

Insights from Work–Life Balance in Dreams

Research by Schredl et al. (2022) delves into the work–life balance as reflected in dreams, underscoring the continuity hypothesis that dreams are continuous with waking life experiences. The study found that hobby-related dreams are more frequent and positively toned compared to work-related dreams, particularly among individuals actively engaging in hobbies. This thematic and emotional continuity supports the notion that dreams reflect waking life priorities and emotional states.

Methodology and Findings

In the study, 1,695 participants were surveyed about their dreams and waking life activities. The findings indicated that hobby-related dreams are more frequent and positively toned compared to work-related dreams, aligning with the continuity hypothesis. Individuals with higher hobby engagement reported more frequent hobby-related dreams, and full-time workers had more work-related dreams than those working part-time or not at all. Emotional continuity was also observed, with work-related emotions influencing the tone of hobby-related dreams, suggesting that waking life emotions are mirrored in dreams independently of dream themes.

Practical Applications of Stable Dreams and Counterbalancing

Dynamic Adjustment in Daily Life

Applying the concept of counterbalancing in daily life involves recognizing when to shift focus between work and personal life. Stable dreams act as subconscious indicators of this need, with the frequency and tone of dreams providing clues about our current balance. By paying attention to dream content, individuals can make conscious adjustments to their waking activities, ensuring a more harmonious balance between work and personal life.

Emotional Awareness and Management

Understanding the emotional continuity between waking life and dreams can help individuals manage stress and emotions more effectively. If work-related stress negatively impacts dream tone, it signals the need for stress management techniques and increased engagement in positive, hobby-related activities. Conversely, positive dream tones can reinforce the benefits of maintaining balanced, fulfilling waking life activities.

The theory of stable dreams and counterbalancing provides a comprehensive framework for understanding the interplay between our waking and subconscious lives. By recognizing the dynamic nature of balance and paying attention to the insights provided by our dreams, we can better navigate the complexities of modern life. Stable dreams not only reflect our waking priorities and emotional states but also guide us towards achieving a more harmonious and fulfilling existence through dynamic, ongoing adjustments.

The Wisdom of Prioritization

Achieving extraordinary results is less about maintaining balance and more about **prioritizing effectively**. This means identifying what is most important in both your professional and personal life and dedicating the necessary time to those priorities. The challenge lies not in avoiding imbalance but in managing it wisely. **Prioritization** allows you to focus deeply on what truly matters, accepting that other areas will receive less attention for a time.

Living an Extraordinary Life

An extraordinary life is not one of perfect balance but one of deliberate, prioritized action. **When you work, work with focus and purpose. When you play, play with joy and presence.** Understanding and embracing the dynamic nature of life, where different priorities take precedence at different times, is key to achieving fulfillment and success.

By embracing the fluid and dynamic process of life integration—much like a well-rehearsed circus performance—you can lead a richer, more fulfilling life. This approach acknowledges the ever-changing demands of life's big top, allowing for periods of intense focus on different areas. Ultimately, this leads to extraordinary accomplishments and a deeper sense of purpose, all while keeping the audience (yourself included) entertained and engaged.

9

Small Is the New Big: How Tiny Triumphs Make Life Gigantic

Do not despise the small beginnings,
for they hold the potential of great endings.

—Lao Tzu

In a world often enamoured by grandeur and magnitude, the adage "small is beautiful" invites us to reconsider the value of the diminutive. This exploration delves into the profound interplay between smallness, goodness, human desires and achievement. We'll investigate how seemingly modest elements can yield profound impacts and why they resonate with us on both cognitive and emotional levels.

The Aesthetics of Miniature

Humans are drawn to small, intricate objects—a delicate seashell, a miniature painting or a bonsai tree. *Why do we find these diminutive creations captivating?* Explore the psychological underpinnings of our aesthetic preferences for small-scale beauty.

Cognitive Ease and Simplicity

Small things often simplify our cognitive load. Consider the joy of a concise poem or a minimalist design. *Investigate how cognitive fluency and ease impact our perception of smallness.*

The Goodness of Small Acts

Acts of Kindness and Micro-Generosity

Small acts of kindness—a smile, holding the door, or a thoughtful note—can have outsized effects. *Analyse the psychological benefits of micro-generosity and its impact on well-being.*

The Butterfly Effect

The butterfly flapping its wings can set off a chain of events. *How do small actions ripple through social networks and influence collective outcomes?* Consider the role of small-scale interventions in promoting positive change.

Human Desires and the Quest for Moderation

The Paradox of Choice

Excessive options overwhelm us. *How does the pursuit of moderation—choosing the "just right" amount—relate to our desires?* Discuss the tension between abundance and contentment.

The Sweet Spot of Ambition

Ambition need not always be grandiose. Sometimes, aiming for smaller, achievable goals leads to greater satisfaction. *Explore the psychology of setting realistic targets and celebrating incremental progress.*

Achievement Beyond Magnitude

The Myth of Bigger Equals Better

Challenge the prevailing notion that bigger achievements are inherently superior. *Highlight cases where small-scale accomplishments have profound significance.*

The Joy of Mastery

Mastery often emerges from deliberate practise, step by step. *How does this relate to the concept of "small is beautiful"?* Discuss the role of incremental improvement in achieving expertise.

The aphorism "small is beautiful and good" invites us to appreciate the subtle, the intricate, and the seemingly insignificant. By embracing the power of smallness, we may discover that greatness lies not only in grand gestures but also in the delicate brushstrokes of everyday life. *Small is good is a truth. It's arguably the most profound truth of all, for if you embrace the modest victories, you'll find contentment and wisdom in your journey.*

Embracing the Petite Achievements

Place the notion of smallness and results in the same vicinity, and people's curiosity piques. Associating the smallness of achievements with success brings to mind simplicity, ease, and clarity. Achievable and straightforward are what sum up their views. Manageable and inviting are what they feel. For some reason, there's a belief that small successes bring enduring joy and peace, that pursuing them enriches time with family and friends, and nurtures health. Confident in their ability to achieve small goals, or motivated by the journey rather than the destination, they feel at ease contemplating it and naturally believe they possess the wisdom for it.

The Love for Small

There is a notion of "comfort-ease" with the concept of small. Let's coin a term for it—microphilia—the rational love for the small. When we associate small with good, it encourages expansive thinking. Elevating our vision feels secure. Embracing where we are feels wise. And the truth is: When small is perceived as good, expansive thinking becomes the norm, and small thrives under its light.

The Intimate Horizon: Lessons From Classical History

Throughout classical history, the human spirit has been driven not just by grand conquests but also by the beauty found in simplicity and small-scale achievements. This journey of discovery and innovation is about recognizing the profound impact of small, deliberate steps in shaping civilizations and inspiring us today. Let's explore this philosophy through powerful examples from classical history, demonstrating how appreciating the small and subtle has shaped our world.

The Humble Mariners: Masters of Their Waters

Voyages of the Phoenicians

The Phoenicians, celebrated for their seafaring skills, embarked on modest yet meaningful voyages across the Mediterranean. Their small but significant expeditions fostered trade and cultural exchange, establishing thriving communities and spreading their influence in a manner that respected and preserved local cultures.

- **Local Trade Networks:** The development of intricate trade routes facilitated not just grand empires but also small, thriving economies.

- **Cultural Preservation:** By focusing on local interactions, they ensured that diverse cultures flourished and enriched each other.

The Intimate Sky: Ancient Astronomy

The Greek Astronomers

Ancient Greek scholars like Ptolemy and Aristarchus made profound contributions to understanding the cosmos through careful, detailed observations rather than grand proclamations.

- **Precision in Observation:** Their meticulous studies laid the groundwork for modern astronomy, proving that detailed, small-scale work can lead to significant advancements.
- **Philosophical Depth:** Their humble approach to the heavens fostered a deep philosophical understanding of humanity's place in the universe.

The Subtle Imagination: Mythology and Invention

The Legends of Daedalus and Icarus

The Greek myth of Daedalus and Icarus symbolizes humanity's desire to transcend limitations through careful, thoughtful invention rather than reckless ambition.

- **Craftsmanship over Ambition:** Daedalus's careful construction of wings represents the beauty of meticulous, small-scale innovation.
- **Cautionary Tales:** Icarus's fall reminds us of the dangers of overreaching, advocating for a balanced approach that values small, deliberate progress.

The Art of Gentle Warfare: Strategic Brilliance

The Strategies of Sun Tzu

In *The Art of War*, Sun Tzu emphasized the power of small, thoughtful actions and adaptability in achieving success.

- **Subtle Tactics:** His teachings highlight the importance of small, strategic moves that accumulate into significant victories.
- **Psychological Insights:** Understanding human nature and leveraging small psychological advantages are key to his strategies.

The Architects of Modest Empires: Vision and Determination

Alexander the Great

Alexander's conquests, while grand, were built on countless small, strategic decisions and respectful cultural integrations.

- **Incremental Integration:** His policy of cultural assimilation was achieved through small, respectful exchanges, fostering a blend of ideas that led to significant advancements.
- **Leadership in Detail:** His leadership style, characterized by attention to detail and small, strategic adjustments, continues to inspire.

Embracing the Art of Mindful Evolution

Historical precedents illustrate that life is about embracing the art of mindful evolution. Like the great figures of the past, we too must recognize that our potential is boundless not in its grandiosity but in the depth of small, meaningful steps. Boundaries may be clear on a map, but in our personal and professional lives, the lines are much subtler. It is this subtle line that signifies our capacity to grow beyond what we perceive as our limits.

Reframing Our Perspective

When asked if thinking small is realistic, the question itself becomes irrelevant when we acknowledge that none of us truly know our ultimate potential. Instead of worrying about setting a grand goal, we should focus on the profound impact of small, deliberate actions. What if we were required to choose a modest threshold below which we could never fall? We would likely choose a sustainable goal, understanding that small, consistent progress is the key to meaningful growth.

The Journey of Small Discoveries

Classical history teaches us that the journey of self-discovery is perpetual and built on small, deliberate steps. Just as ancient mariners, astronomers, inventors, strategists and empire builders shaped their world through meticulous, thoughtful actions, we must embrace the power of the small. Our capacity for growth is as intimate as the horizon itself, and our journey, like theirs, is one of continuous, mindful evolution.

The Leap of Simplicity

In this context, small is a placeholder for what you might call a leap of simplicity. It's the office assistant visualizing the quiet life or a humble artisan imagining a small but meaningful impact. It's about modest ideas that respect your comfort zones while reflecting your most profound opportunities. Believing in small helps you to ask simpler questions, follow simpler paths, and try humble things. This opens doors to possibilities that until now only lived quietly within you.

The Charm of Small Beginnings: Stories of Incremental Success

The philosophy that "small is beautiful" is beautifully exemplified through the journeys of several visionaries who embraced modest beginnings and achieved significant impact. Their stories highlight the power of small, incremental steps in building substantial success.

J.K. Rowling: The Power of a Modest Start

Humble Beginnings

J.K. Rowling's journey to success began with a simple idea scribbled on a napkin. With no grand plans or substantial financial backing, she started writing *Harry Potter* while living on welfare.

- **Incremental Writing:** Rowling wrote the first book in cafés during her daughter's naps, focusing on crafting a single, compelling story.
- **Persistence and Patience:** She faced multiple rejections from publishers but remained committed to her modest yet impactful goal.

Gradual Success

Her first book, *Harry Potter and the Philosopher's Stone,* was initially printed in a limited run of 500 copies. However, its success grew steadily through word of mouth.

- **Organic Growth:** The book's popularity spread gradually, leading to a series that has sold over 500 million copies worldwide.

- **Cultural Impact:** Rowling's modest start has had a massive cultural impact, inspiring readers and aspiring writers globally.

Steve Wozniak: The Small Start of a Tech Giant

Early Days of Apple

Steve Wozniak, co-founder of Apple Inc., began his journey with a simple goal: To build affordable personal computers. Working in a garage, he focused on creating a small, functional computer that could be accessible to everyone.

- **Basic Innovation:** Wozniak's first prototype, the Apple I, was a modest machine that demonstrated the potential of personal computing.
- **Small-Scale Production:** Initial production runs were limited, with each unit assembled by hand.

Building Momentum

The success of the Apple I led to the development of the Apple II, which became one of the first highly successful mass-produced personal computers.

- **Steady Expansion:** Wozniak's incremental improvements and focus on user-friendly design helped Apple grow into a tech giant.
- **Enduring Legacy:** His approach of starting small and refining the product has influenced countless tech innovations.

Yvon Chouinard: Crafting a Sustainable Brand

The Birth of Patagonia

Yvon Chouinard started Patagonia with a modest goal: To create high-quality climbing gear. Operating out of his car, he began by selling hand-forged climbing equipment to fellow enthusiasts.

- **Handcrafted Beginnings:** Each piece of equipment was crafted with care, focusing on durability and functionality.
- **Sustainable Practices:** Chouinard's commitment to small-scale, sustainable production set the foundation for Patagonia's ethos.

Growing with Purpose

Patagonia's reputation for quality grew through word of mouth, and the company expanded gradually without compromising its values.

- **Community Focus:** By prioritizing environmental sustainability and ethical practices, Patagonia built a loyal customer base.
- **Impactful Growth:** Today, Patagonia is a leading outdoor brand, proving that small, purpose-driven beginnings can lead to substantial success.

Jamie Oliver: Transforming Food Culture One Recipe at a Time

Simple Start in Cooking

Jamie Oliver began his career as a chef with a simple mission: to make cooking accessible and enjoyable for everyone. His initial television show, *The Naked Chef,* focused on straightforward, easy-to-follow recipes.

- **Basic Recipes:** Oliver's approach was to simplify cooking, making it approachable for people with varying skill levels.

- **Authentic Presentation:** His genuine, down-to-earth style resonated with viewers, fostering a strong connection.

Expanding Influence

Oliver's modest start in television evolved into a global culinary empire, including cookbooks, restaurants and food-advocacy initiatives.

- **Gradual Expansion:** His influence grew through consistent, small steps—one recipe, one show, one book at a time.
- **Public Health Impact:** Oliver's focus on healthy eating and food education has had a lasting impact on public health and nutrition awareness.

These stories illustrate that starting small can lead to significant achievements. J.K. Rowling, Steve Wozniak, Yvon Chouinard, and Jamie Oliver all embraced the philosophy that "small is beautiful," focusing on modest beginnings and incremental growth. Their journeys remind us that small, thoughtful steps can build a foundation for enduring success, proving that grand dreams can be realized through the power of small, meaningful actions.

The Essence of Thinking Small

Thinking small is essential to sustainable results. Success requires action, and action requires thought. But here's the catch—the only actions that lead to enduring success are those informed by modest thinking from the outset. Make this connection, and the importance of thinking small becomes clear.

Everyone has the same amount of time, and focused work is simply focused work. Therefore, what you achieve is determined by what you do in the time you work. And since what you do is determined by what you think, how small you think becomes the foundation for how effectively you achieve.

The Ladder of Modest Success

Think of it this way: every level of achievement requires its own combination of what you do, how you do it, and who you do it with. The trouble is that the combination that gets you to one level of success won't naturally evolve to the next level. Doing something one way doesn't always lay the foundation for doing something better, nor does a relationship with one person automatically set the stage for a more effective relationship with another. It's unfortunate, but these things don't build on each other. If you learn to do something one way, and with one set of relationships, that may work fine until you want to achieve more. It's then that you'll discover you've created an artificial ceiling of achievement for yourself that may be too hard to break through. In effect, you've boxed yourself in. To avoid this, think as small as you reasonably can and base what you do, how you do it, and who you do it with on succeeding at that level. It might take you more than a lifetime to reach the boundaries of a box this small.

> *Great things are not done by impulse, but by a series of small things brought together.*
>
> —Vincent Van Gogh

The Humble Path

Starting with easy questions can be surprisingly helpful. At first glance, small goals might not seem significant. However, think about the times you've started something that seemed daunting but turned out to be much easier than anticipated. Sometimes tasks are harder than expected, and other times, they're simpler. It's crucial to remember that you grow incrementally as you work towards small goals. Embracing smallness requires humility, and by the time you reach your goal, you've learned to appreciate simplicity. From a distance, what appeared to be a minor task can become a manageable endeavour once you're up close—especially compared to the person you've become along the way. Transitioning from big to small alters your thinking, skills, relationships and perceptions of what is achievable and what it entails.

As you experience small, you become humbler.

When Blake Mycoskie, founder of TOMS Shoes, began building his team, he emphasized the importance of small, meaningful actions. He believed that minor, consistent efforts could accumulate into significant impact, echoing the philosophy of Norman Vincent Peale. Mycoskie's vision was simple yet profound: For every pair of shoes sold, a new pair would be given to a child in need.

Embracing Incremental Progress

Mycoskie's approach to business was grounded in the idea that small actions can lead to substantial results. He encouraged his team to focus on manageable, incremental goals rather than overwhelming ambitions.

- **Learning through Small Steps:** Mycoskie emphasized the importance of learning from small-scale initiatives and gradually expanding the impact of their efforts.
- **Incremental Improvement:** By starting with a simple, clear mission, TOMS was able to grow steadily, building a strong foundation for future success.

Building a Foundation for Success

Mycoskie's strategy highlighted the importance of maintaining a positive outlook and a growth mindset, principles that Norman Vincent Peale championed.

- **Recruiting the Right Mindset:** Mycoskie selected team members who believed in the power of small actions and were committed to making a difference, one step at a time.
- **Cultivating a Positive Environment:** By fostering an environment that valued incremental progress and small wins, TOMS was able to stay focused and motivated.

The Outcome: Transformative Impact

The significance of Mycoskie's approach became evident in the remarkable success and social impact of TOMS Shoes.

- **Innovative Social Enterprise:** TOMS grew from a simple idea into a global movement, providing millions of shoes to children in need and inspiring other businesses to adopt similar models.
- **Enduring Legacy:** The success of TOMS serves as a testament to the power of small actions and the growth mindset, principles that continue to inspire social entrepreneurship and positive change.

Blake Mycoskie's leadership and vision, inspired by the philosophy of Norman Vincent Peale, demonstrate the profound impact of small actions. By embracing incremental progress, fostering a growth mindset, and maintaining a positive environment, TOMS achieved remarkable success and social impact. This story reminds us that small, thoughtful steps can lead to significant, lasting achievements and transformative change.

Enriching Your Life

Small stands for contentment—sustainable results. Pursue a small life, and you're pursuing the most meaningful life you can possibly live. To live meaningfully, you have to think small. You must be open to the possibility that your life and what you accomplish can be modest yet profound. Achievement and fulfilment show up because they're the natural outcomes of doing the right things with no grand ambitions attached.

Fearing the Wrong Thing

Don't fear small. Fear overambition. Fear waste. Fear the lack of living to your fullest. When we fear small, we either consciously or subconsciously work against it. We either run towards grandiose outcomes and opportunities or simply run away from the small ones. If wisdom isn't the absence of folly but moving past it, then thinking small isn't the absence of doubts but moving past them. Only living small will let you experience your true life and work potential.

Embracing Small Ideas

1. **Small Is Beautiful:** Small ideas, gifts and actions might seem insignificant at first, but they hold the potential to be transformative. By embracing incremental thinking, we recognize the power of simplicity and appreciate each small step forward, creating a quick path to contentment. Simplifying our goals by setting smaller, more attainable targets makes the journey to success more manageable and almost guarantees achievement. Small actions build a solid foundation for larger accomplishments, and thoughtful

gestures can significantly enhance relationships and well-being. Focusing on manageable tasks reduces burnout and maintains steady progress, fuelling motivation and engagement with each small victory. Mindful attention to life's little details keeps us present, enhances happiness, and reduces stress. Embracing small things doesn't mean settling for less; it means valuing every step and appreciating the journey as much as the destination, setting the stage for sustainable success and lasting contentment.

2. **Act Humbly:** Why bother with grand ambitions if your actions don't reflect them? Ponder a simple question and picture life without the answer. If you can't see it clearly, look to those who have failed. While we might like to believe we're the same, what fails for others often fails for us too.

3. **Embrace Small Blessings:** Success is about achieving your goals and celebrating every step along the way. Embrace a mindset that appreciates each small victory, no matter how minor it may seem. Meaningful results are built on these consistent successes. There's no need to avoid challenges; instead, recognize and celebrate each accomplishment. Every small success is a stepping stone to greater achievements.

PART TWO

RE-DETOX
The Vulnerability Essentialism

To be yourself in a world that is constantly trying to make you something else is the greatest accomplishment.

—Ralph Waldo Emerson

The Simple Path to Productivity

In the world of tech and innovation, many successful figures have shared their journeys of embracing simplicity and authenticity to achieve extraordinary results. Here are some insights drawn from their experiences.

Steve Jobs, co-founder of Apple, once said, "Simple can be harder than complex: You have to work hard to get your thinking clean to make it simple." Jobs understood that focusing on the essentials and eliminating the unnecessary could lead to remarkable innovation. His emphasis on simplicity was evident in Apple's products, which were known for their sleek design and user-friendly interface.

In my own pursuit of success, I initially believed that everything mattered equally. Like Jobs, I thought cramming my schedule with tasks would lead to greater achievements. However, this approach only led to frustration and self-doubt. I realized that, like Apple's focus on core products, I needed to identify and concentrate on the most crucial aspects of my work.

Arianna Huffington, founder of *The Huffington Post* (now *HuffPost*), experienced a wake-up call when she collapsed from exhaustion. This incident led her to re-evaluate her approach to work and success. She began prioritizing sleep, well-being and mindfulness, which ultimately enhanced her productivity and satisfaction.

I, too, faced a breaking point where the constant tension and stress took a toll on my health. Inspired by Huffington's transformation, I started listening to my body, slowing down and incorporating wellness practices into my routine. This shift allowed me to maintain a healthier balance and achieve greater success without sacrificing my well-being.

Brené Brown, a researcher and storyteller, has emphasized the power of vulnerability and authenticity. She argues that embracing our true selves and letting go of the need to fit a specific mold can lead to deeper connections and more meaningful achievements.

For a long time, I believed I had to project an image of success—talking, walking, and dressing the part. However, this façade was exhausting and unfulfilling. Inspired by Brown's teachings, I began to drop the pretense and return to my authentic self. I found that being true to who I am not only brought me greater peace but also led to more genuine success.

Greg McKeown, author of *Essentialism*, advocates for the disciplined pursuit of less but better. He encourages individuals to identify what is truly essential and to focus their energy on those few key priorities.

In my quest for success, I initially tried to do everything, believing that more effort would lead to greater results. However, this approach only led to burnout. Inspired by McKeown's philosophy, I started doing less—intentionally and purposefully. By focusing on a few essential tasks, I found that I could achieve much more with less effort.

Embracing the philosophy of re-detox invites us to periodically cleanse our lives of the clutter and noise that naturally accumulate. This transformative approach includes regular reflection to discern what truly adds value and what merely distracts, purposeful purging of unnecessary tasks, commitments, and relationships that do not nurture our well-being or goals, and the incorporation of mindful practices to maintain mental clarity and focus. By weaving RE-DETOX into my life, I consistently reassessed my priorities and streamlined my focus, allowing me to stay aligned with my true purpose and gracefully avoid burnout.

Brené Brown shows us how to celebrate vulnerability as a powerful strength that nurtures genuine connection and authenticity. This approach encourages us to embrace imperfection, recognizing that mistakes and failures are integral to growth. It promotes authentic communication, urging us to be open and honest in our interactions to build trust and forge deeper relationships. It also calls for courageous choices, guiding us to make decisions that reflect our true values and beliefs, even when challenging. By embracing Vulnerability Essentialism, I learned to share my struggles openly and live more authentically, both professionally and personally, leading to deeper connections and a more fulfilling success.

These tales of real-life luminaries illuminate the profound impact of simplicity, well-being, authenticity and essentialism. From them, I gleaned invaluable lessons: To embrace authenticity and be true to oneself, as Brené Brown so passionately advocates, for it nurtures deeper connections and a more meaningful success; to prioritize well-being, drawing inspiration from Arianna Huffington, by embedding mindfulness, rest and balance into daily life; and to focus on essentials, as Greg McKeown advises, by honing in on what truly matters and excelling in those areas. By weaving these principles into the fabric of my life, I embarked on a journey toward success and fulfillment greater than I ever imagined. This, I discovered, is the beautifully simple truth behind achieving greatness.

10

Ask Away Anyway

Focusing on what truly matters while discarding the superfluous is a refined skill that is both simple and versatile. It requires the courage to view things from a new perspective.

—Marie Kondo

Always Ask when in Doubt

On March 18, 2022, in Austin, Texas, Elon Musk addressed the employees of Tesla and SpaceX. At the peak of his business success, Musk's ventures stood as the most innovative and influential in the automotive and aerospace industries. Eventually, Musk would be recognized as one of the richest individuals in modern history. In his speech titled "The Road to Technological Success," Musk shared his journey as a prosperous entrepreneur and imparted this crucial advice:

> The fundamental condition of success—the great secret—is to concentrate your energy, thoughts and resources solely on the mission you are passionate about. Having embarked on a path, commit to it unwaveringly. Lead it, adopt every innovation, acquire the best technology, and become the most knowledgeable about it. Failures arise from those

who disperse their resources and, consequently, their focus. They have interests scattered across various ventures. The adage "Don't put all your eggs in one basket" is erroneous. Instead, put all your eggs in one basket and vigilantly safeguard that basket. Observe your surroundings; those who do this seldom fail. It is manageable to oversee and carry one basket. Attempting to manage multiple baskets leads to the breaking of eggs.

He advised one to ask one's doubt away constantly!

This advice reflects several key theories:

- **Resource Focus Theory**: The focused approach ensures that resources are maximized and not wasted on less important tasks. By concentrating efforts on asking for the high-priority areas, organizations can optimize the use of their human, financial and technological resources. This theory emphasizes the importance of strategic allocation, reducing redundancies, and eliminating tasks that do not contribute significantly to the organization's objectives. By maintaining a clear focus, companies can achieve greater efficiency and effectiveness, ultimately leading to better outcomes and higher productivity.
- **Focused Investment Theory:** Concentrated investments yield higher returns compared to diversified, unfocused investments. This theory posits that by channelling resources into select, high-potential opportunities, investors and organizations can achieve superior financial performance. Focused investments allow for a deeper understanding of the chosen ventures, leading to better management and oversight. This approach reduces the dilution of resources and ensures that efforts are directed towards the most

promising areas, thereby maximizing returns and minimizing risks associated with spreading resources too thin.

- **Opportunity Cost Analysis:** Prioritizing one task over others highlights the importance of choosing the most impactful task. Opportunity cost analysis involves evaluating the potential benefits of different actions and selecting the one that offers the greatest return on investment. By understanding the trade-offs involved in decision-making, organizations can make informed choices that align with their strategic goals. This analytical approach helps to identify the true cost of forgone alternatives, ensuring that resources are allocated to initiatives that provide the highest value and long-term benefits.
- **Behavioural Decision Economics:** Clear, well-posed questions lead to better decisions and outcomes. This field of study examines how cognitive biases and heuristics influence decision-making processes. By framing questions and choices in a manner that minimizes biases, organizations can improve the quality of their decisions. Behavioural decision economics emphasizes the importance of simplicity, clarity and context in presenting options to decision-makers. Understanding human behaviour and psychological factors can lead to more rational and effective decision-making, enhancing overall performance and achieving desired results.
- **Business Structure Theory:** Focused management leads to more efficient operations and higher profitability. This theory explores how organizational design and management practices impact business performance. By implementing a focused management approach, companies can streamline their operations, reduce complexity, and enhance coordination among different functions. A well-structured organization with clear roles, responsibilities and communication channels can operate more smoothly,

respond to changes more rapidly, and achieve higher levels of profitability. Effective management structures foster a culture of accountability, innovation, and continuous improvement, driving sustainable growth and success.

*It were not best that we should all think alike;
it is difference of opinion that makes horse races.*

—Mark Twain

The Catalyst of Inquiry

Why focus on questions when we just want answers? Simple: Answers come from questions, and a great question leads to a great answer. If you ask a question like "Why is the sky blue?" you'll get a solid answer. But if you ask, "Why is my cat plotting to overthrow me?" well, good luck with that. The right question can change everything.

While answers provide closure, it is the art of questioning that propels discovery forward. By posing questions, we unlock new realms of understanding, with the depth and precision of our questions shaping the quality of the insights we gain. Major advancements are often the result of a single, profound question that sparks innovation. Trailblazers and visionaries begin their explorations with a crucial question that sets their course. The scientific method, grounded in the creation of hypotheses, illustrates this continuous search for knowledge.

Sir Francis Bacon dropped this wisdom bomb: *"A prudent question is one-half of wisdom."* And Indira Gandhi? She knew what's up, saying, *"The power to question is the basis of all human progress."* Exceptional questions pave the way to exceptional answers. Every trailblazer and inventor starts their journey with a game-changing question. The scientific method itself is all about asking the universe **"What if?"** in the form of hypotheses. For over two thousand years, the Socratic Method has proven the educational power of questioning, benefiting learners from elite universities to local schools. Thoughtful questioning enhances our analytical skills.

Questions are like mental push-ups for our brains. Studies show that asking questions can boost learning and performance by up to 150 per cent. It's like upgrading your brain's software. The essence of life as a question is encapsulated in these lines: "Any wage I had asked of Life, Life would have willingly paid."

Think of the Buddha, who sat under the Bodhi tree not just seeking enlightenment, but asking profound questions about the nature of suffering and existence. His journey was driven by questions like, "Why do we suffer?" and "What is the path to true happiness?" These potent inquiries led to his enlightenment and the wisdom that transformed millions of lives. One of the most empowering realizations is that life is a question and our answers shape our existence. The way we frame our questions dictates the answers that define our lives. So next time you're scratching your head, remember: The right question might just be your ticket to enlightenment—or at least to finding out why your cat is giving you that suspicious look.

The Anatomy of the Question

Alright, folks, gather around for the secret sauce to success—the Real Question! Imagine a magic wand that turns your chaotic to-do list into a streamlined path to greatness. This nifty little question boils down all those pesky inquiries into one laser-focused gem: "What's THAT QUESTION? By it, will everything else be easier?"

11

Fail Hard, Win Big: The Secret Sauce of Top Achievers

Every adversity, every failure, every heartache carries with it the seed of a greater or equal benefit.

—Napoleon Hill

Embracing Failure: A Modern Guide to Success

The Routine of Failure

Routines are the invisible architecture of our daily lives. They can be stubborn to change, yet we continually form new ones, often without even noticing. Creating beneficial routines can be daunting, but in the modern world, a pivotal routine is learning to embrace failure. This guide aims to transform our perception of failure, illustrating why failing frequently is not only beneficial but essential for growth and achievement in today's fast-paced environment.

The Necessity of Failure

Imagine a world where every misstep was celebrated as a step forward. Failure shouldn't be seen as a setback; it's a necessity. Through our failures, we gain the most valuable insights, uncovering innovative solutions and new directions. Embracing failure encourages risk-taking and experimentation, and ultimately leads to success in ways that were previously unimaginable.

The Iteration Principle

In the tech industry, iteration is the cornerstone of development. Companies like Google and Apple thrive on constantly improving their products, learning from each iteration's shortcomings. This principle is equally applicable to personal growth. By viewing each failure as an iteration, we can refine our skills, strategies, and approaches.

The Growth Mindset

Psychologist Carol Dweck's growth mindset theory asserts that abilities and intelligence can be developed through dedication and hard work. A growth mindset perceives failure as a crucial part of the learning process, not a dead-end.

Example: Michael Jordan, one of the greatest basketball players of all time, was cut from his high school basketball team. Instead of giving up, he used that failure as motivation to improve, which led to his extraordinary career.

The Failure Resume

Economist Johannes Haushofer popularized the concept of a failure resume—a catalogue of one's biggest failures. This practice normalizes failure and encourages introspection on the lessons learned from each experience.

Example: Haushofer's own failure resume includes rejected job applications, unsuccessful research proposals and other setbacks. By publicly sharing these failures, he emphasizes that failure is a universal experience and a necessary component of success.

The Introverted Innovators

Introverts often face unique challenges, but their reflective nature can turn failure into a powerful tool for innovation. Introverted individuals tend to analyse their failures deeply, leading to profound insights and improvements.

Example: J.K. Rowling, the renowned author of the Harry Potter series, faced numerous rejections from publishers before her books became a global phenomenon. Her introverted nature allowed her to persevere, refining her story until it captivated millions.

Authors and Their Missteps

Famous authors frequently encounter failure, often using it as a stepping stone to greater success. The literary world is rife with stories of initial rejection and later acclaim.

Example: Stephen King's first novel, *Carrie*, was rejected 30 times before it was published. King even threw the manuscript in the trash, but his wife retrieved it and encouraged him to keep trying. The book's eventual success launched his prolific career.

Strategies to Embrace Failure

1. **Reframe Your Perspective:** View failures as valuable lessons rather than defeats. Each failure provides insights that bring you closer to your goals.
2. **Set Process Goals:** Instead of focusing solely on outcome goals, set process goals that emphasize effort and learning. This shift can reduce the fear of failure and encourage continuous improvement.
3. **Create a Safe Space for Failure:** Whether in the workplace or personal projects, create environments where failure is

accepted and even celebrated. Encourage risk-taking and innovation by allowing room for mistakes.
4. **Reflect and Learn:** After each failure, take time to reflect on what went wrong and what can be improved. This practice turns each failure into a stepping stone for future success.
5. **Share Your Failures:** Normalize failure by sharing your experiences with others. This can help build a supportive community that understands the importance of failing forward.

Real-Life Examples of Embracing Failure

Introverted Success Stories

1. **Albert Einstein:** Known for his reflective and introverted nature, Einstein faced numerous academic failures early in life. His unique approach to failure allowed him to develop groundbreaking theories that changed the world.
2. **Bill Gates:** An introvert who dropped out of Harvard, Gates faced several business failures before founding Microsoft. His introspective nature helped him learn from these failures and build one of the most successful tech companies in the world.

Failure is not just a part of the journey; it's a vital component of success. By embracing failure, we open ourselves up to endless possibilities and continuous growth. Remember, it's not about how many times we fail but how we respond to and learn from those failures that defines our path to success. So, fail often, fail boldly, and watch as each failure propels you towards your greatest achievements.

Golden Nuggets

Why Failures Are a Must and Necessary

Alright, let's dive into the wonderfully chaotic world of embracing failure! How do you make failing forward part of your daily routine, turning your mishaps into stepping stones for extraordinary results at work and in life? Buckle up, because here's a fun and extensive guide based on our wild experiences and the wisdom we've gathered.

Fail Frequently: Learning from Real-World Examples

Academics: Dr Seuss

Before becoming a beloved children's author, Dr Seuss (Theodor Geisel) faced numerous rejections from publishers. His first book, *And to Think That I Saw It on Mulberry Street,* was rejected 27 times before it was finally published. Geisel's persistence and creativity paid off, and he went on to write some of the most popular children's books of all time, such as *The Cat in the Hat and Green Eggs and Ham.* His initial failures were crucial in honing his craft and eventually leading to his extraordinary success in children's literature

Entertainment: Steven Spielberg

Even Steven Spielberg, one of the most successful directors in film history, was rejected from the University of Southern California's film school multiple times. He didn't let these rejections stop him. Instead, he found other ways to hone his craft, eventually creating some of the most iconic movies of all time.

Politics: Abraham Lincoln

Abraham Lincoln faced multiple failures before becoming one of the most revered presidents of the United States. He lost numerous elections, faced business failures, and dealt with personal tragedies. Each setback was a lesson that shaped his resilience and leadership.

Sports: Michael Jordan

Michael Jordan, often regarded as the greatest basketball player of all time, didn't make his high school varsity basketball team on his first try. Instead of giving up, he used this failure as fuel to work harder, eventually becoming a legend in the sport.

Turn Failing into a Habit

Tech Industry: Elon Musk

Elon Musk's journey with SpaceX and Tesla is filled with failures, from rockets exploding to cars that didn't meet expectations. However, Musk embraces these failures, viewing them as opportunities to learn and improve. His persistence has led to revolutionary advancements in space travel and electric vehicles.

Business: Oprah Winfrey

Oprah Winfrey faced numerous setbacks early in her career, including being fired from her first television job. She turned these failures into stepping stones, eventually building a media empire and becoming an influential figure in the world of entertainment and business.

Get Cozy with Failure

Medicine: Dr Robert Jarvik

Dr Robert Jarvik, inventor of the first permanent artificial heart, faced countless failures and rejections before achieving success. His ability to view failure as a necessary part of the innovation process led to life-saving medical advancements.

Innovation: Thomas Edison

Thomas Edison famously said, "I have not failed. I've just found 10,000 ways that won't work." His relentless experimentation and comfort with failure eventually led to the invention of the electric light bulb, transforming modern life.

Use Fun Reminders

Education: Failure Walls

Some schools and universities have started using "Failure Walls," where students and staff post their failures and what they've learned from them. This practice helps normalize failure as part of the learning process, fostering a culture of resilience and growth.

Corporate World: Failure Celebrations

Companies like Google and Pixar hold regular "failure celebrations," where employees share their biggest failures and the lessons learned. These celebrations encourage a culture of innovation and continuous improvement.

12

Pause, Reflect and Just Chill

Take a deep breath, and remind yourself that you are the only person you can control.

—Oprah Winfrey

Sometimes, burnout hits us like a ton of bricks—whether from excessive work, stress, or failing to balance work and life. When this happens, it's essential to take a step back, find some peace, and dedicate time to yourself. Let's take a leaf out of Ferris Bueller's book: "Life moves pretty fast. If you don't stop and look around once in a while, you could miss it." So, let's explore the art of taking breaks, going on epic adventures, indulging in hobbies, and unplugging from the social media frenzy.

Strategies to Double Your Fun

Plan an Epic Adventure:

- Map out a road trip or backpacking journey.
- Explore new places, meet quirky people and create unforgettable memories.

Unplug and Unwind:

- Schedule regular social media detoxes.
- Swap screen time for joy-inducing activities like reading, gardening or even painting (not your cat's nails, though).

Join a New Class:

- Enroll in a dance, cooking or pottery class.
- Learning something new can be hilariously fulfilling and fun.

Host Regular Gatherings:

- Plan monthly game nights or themed dinner parties.
- Social interactions can rejuvenate your spirit and provide endless laughter.

Focus on Wellness:

- Incorporate yoga, meditation or a fitness routine into your daily life.
- Physical well-being boosts mental health and overall happiness. Plus, who doesn't love a good stretch?

Anne Lamott nailed it: "Almost everything will work again if you unplug it for a few minutes…including you."

So, take that break, come back with more energy, creativity and joy. Double your fun, dodge burnout, and live life to the fullest!

Psychologist-Recommended Exercises for Burnout

Mindfulness and Meditation: Dr Jon Kabat-Zinn, creator of the Mindfulness-Based Stress Reduction programme, highlights that mindfulness helps manage stress by keeping you present. Practising mindfulness can reduce anxiety and depression, improve attention, and increase overall well-being.

Exercise:

1. Find a quiet place.
2. Sit comfortably and close your eyes.
3. Focus on your breathing.
4. If your mind wanders, gently bring it back to your breath.
5. Start with five minutes daily, gradually increasing to 20 minutes.

Physical Activity: Dr John Ratey, author of *Spark: The Revolutionary New Science of Exercise and the Brain,* emphasizes that exercise improves mood, reduces anxiety, and increases cognitive function.

Exercise:

1. Choose an activity you enjoy (walking, jogging, cycling).
2. Aim for at least 30 minutes of moderate exercise most days of the week.
3. Incorporate variety to keep it interesting (yoga, swimming, dance).

Creative Hobbies: Dr Teresa Amabile, professor at Harvard Business School, notes that creativity enhances problem-solving skills and can lead to a more fulfilling life.

Exercise:

1. Identify a hobby that excites you (painting, writing, cooking).
2. Set aside regular time each week to indulge in your hobby.

PART THREE

THE LAW OF ATTRACTION
Unlocking Your Inner Dreams

Success is not final, failure is not fatal:
It is the courage to continue that counts.

—Winston Churchill

Unlocking PURPOSE follows a natural rhythm in our lives, governed by dreams, priority and productivity. These three elements intertwine, each validating and reinforcing the others, guiding us toward fulfillment and achievement.

Your dream, the big ONE Thing, sets the course for your journey. It acts as a magnetic north, directing your efforts toward meaningful objectives. From purpose emerges priority—the small one goal—a singular focus that propels you forward. Successful individuals align their actions with dream-driven priorities, charting the most direct route to success.

Think of purpose, priority, and productivity as facets of the Law of Attraction. Like different types of attraction, they attract and shape visible outcomes, much like an iceberg where what's seen above water is influenced by what lies beneath—purpose and priority.

In business, the synergy between productivity and profit reflects purposeful priorities. While productivity and profit are the visible outcomes sought by all, their sustainability hinges on the foundational elements of purpose and priority. Businesses flourish when guided by purposeful priorities, building success incrementally through productive actions.

Ultimately, the harmonious alignment of purpose, priority and productivity distinguishes exceptional individuals and thriving enterprises. This understanding embodies the essence of achieving extraordinary results.

13

Crafting an Extraordinary Life

Your work is going to fill a large part of your life, and the only way to be truly satisfied is to do what you believe is great work. And the only way to do great work is to love what you do.

—Steve Jobs

There is hardly anyone who doesn't crave and dream of an extraordinary life? Regina George shows us how. Cold-hearted, manipulative and vain, a girl who despised anyone who threatened her popularity and all things that give people genuine happiness, her name a byword for cruelty and superficiality—Regina George might have been the least likely candidate to teach us anything about how to live. Yet, in the 2004 movie *Mean Girls* she does.

The redemptive tale of Regina's transformation from mean-spirited, conniving and unloved to considerate, caring and beloved is one of the best examples of how our destinies are determined by our decisions, our lives shaped by our choices. Once again, fiction provides us with a formula we can all follow to build an extraordinary life with extraordinary results. I'd like to beg your forgiveness, take a little cinematic license, and quickly retell this timeless tale to show you.

One fateful Halloween, Regina George is confronted by a series of events that make her reflect on her actions. She doesn't know if it's a dream or if it's real. She gets a glimpse into her past, present and future—thanks to some unexpected and mysterious guidance. "I am here tonight to warn you that you have yet a chance and a hope of escaping your fate. You will be haunted by three spirits"—from the past, present and future, as it turns out. "Remember what has passed between us!"

Now, let's stop for a second and bear in mind who Regina is. She is the queen bee of North Shore High, known for her biting sarcasm, manipulation and control over her peers. She rules with an iron fist, and everyone fears her. She is secretive and solitary, surrounded by a clique that's more about status than genuine friendship. No one ever approaches her with sincere affection. No one cares, for she cares for no one. She is a bitter, mean, covetous young woman—cold to the sight, cold to the touch, and cold of heart, with no thaw in sight. Her life is a lonely existence, and the world is worse off for it.

Over the course of the night, the three spirits visit Regina to show her her past, present and future. Through these visits, she sees how she became the girl she is, how her life is currently going, and what will ultimately happen to her and those around her. It's a terrifying experience that leaves her visibly shaken when she wakes the next morning. Not knowing whether it was real or a dream, but giddy upon discovering no time has passed, Regina realizes there is still time to alter her fate. In a joyous blur, she rushes to school and does something unexpected: she apologizes to the people she's hurt. She helps a classmate she once ridiculed with her math homework and even invites her former victims to sit with her at lunch.

Regina eventually ends up reconciling with her former friends, where she begs forgiveness for being such a fool for far too long and accepts an invitation to join them in their genuine, heartfelt gatherings. Her friends, shocked at her heartfelt bliss, can barely believe this is Regina.

The next morning, Regina arrives at school with a new attitude, ready to make amends. When a student, previously bullied by her, timidly approaches, Regina greets her with kindness and offers her help. The entire school is astounded by the transformation.

Regina goes on to become a supportive and beloved member of the school community. She starts a peer support group, helps organize charity events, and becomes an advocate for kindness and inclusivity.

Through this simple story, *Mean Girls* shows us a simple formula for creating an extraordinary life: Live with purpose. Live by priority. Live for productivity.

As I reflect on this story, I believe it reveals purpose as a combination of where we're going and what's important to us. It implies that our priority is what we place the greatest importance on, and our productivity comes from the actions we take. It lays out life as a series of connected choices, where our purpose sets our priority, and our priority determines the productivity our actions produce.

Our purpose determines who we are.

Regina is transparent and easy to understand, so let's revisit *Mean Girls* through the lens of this formula. At the place we enter her life, Regina's purpose is clearly about maintaining her status and power. She pursues a life either manipulating for it or being alone with it. She cares for status more than for people and believes that popularity is the end by which any means are justified. Based on her purpose, her priority is straightforward: Maintaining her power and control. Gossiping, manipulating, backstabbing—these are the actions that fill her days, for she is selfish and unmoved by the human condition of those around her.

By Regina's own standards, she's highly productive in accomplishing her purpose. By anyone else's, it's simply a miserable life.

This would be the end of the story, were it not for the perspective provided to Regina by her mysterious guides. They didn't want Regina to reach the same dead end they had. So, after the haunting, what happened to Regina? Her purpose changed, which changed her most important priority, which changed where she focused her productivity. After the intervention, Regina experienced the transformative power of a new purpose.

So, who did she become? Well, let's look.

As the narrative ends, Regina's purpose is no longer about power, but about people. She now cares about people. She cares about their feelings and their well-being. She sees herself happily in relationships with others, lending a hand in any way she can. She values helping people more than maintaining status and believes popularity is good for the good it can do.

What do we learn from this? Where she once saved face and used people, she now uses her influence to save people. Her overriding priority is to make as many genuine connections as she can, so she can help as many as she can. Her actions? She is productive throughout her days putting every effort into being kind and supportive.

The transformation is remarkable, *the message unmistakable.* Who we are and where we want to go determine what we do and what we accomplish. A life lived on purpose is the most powerful of all—and the happiest.

Unlocking True Self-Worth through Self-Actualization

When people are asked about their greatest desire in life, "fulfillment" frequently tops the list. Despite its widespread appeal, fulfillment remains an elusive and misunderstood goal. Many of our efforts are focused on attaining it, yet we often miss the target. True fulfillment doesn't arrive in the ways we anticipate.

The Clever Fox and the Endless Journey

Once upon a time, in a dense and magical forest, a sly fox named Fable roamed with a keen eye for opportunities. One sunny afternoon, while resting beneath a sprawling oak tree, Fable noticed a wise old tortoise slowly making its way across the forest floor.

"Where are you going, old friend?" asked Fable, curious about the tortoise's destination.

The tortoise, named Sage, looked up and replied with a knowing smile, "I am on a journey to find the Everlasting Fountain of Wisdom."

Intrigued and always looking for an adventure, Fable said, "Let me accompany you! With my speed and your wisdom, we will reach the fountain in no time."

Sage, with a twinkle in his eye, responded, "Very well, but remember, this journey is not as simple as it seems."

Excited and confident, Fable set off with Sage, believing that the journey would be quick and the reward great. They crossed rivers, climbed hills, and navigated through dense woods. Days turned into weeks, and Fable began to grow impatient. Every time they thought they were close, the path seemed to stretch on endlessly.

"How much longer must we travel, Sage?" Fable complained. "It feels like we are going in circles!"

Sage chuckled softly and said, "Patience, my friend. The journey itself holds the lessons you seek."

Determined not to give up, Fable pressed on. As they journeyed, Fable started to notice the beauty of the forest—the vibrant flowers, the melodious birds, and the serenity of the flowing streams. The fox began to appreciate the company of Sage and the wisdom he shared during their travels.

One evening, as they sat by a campfire, Fable asked, "Sage, what is the true purpose of this journey? I feel like I have learned so much already."

Sage smiled and replied, "You see, the Everlasting Fountain of Wisdom is not a place you reach, but a state of being. The journey we undertake is endless because true wisdom comes from the experiences we gather and the insights we gain along the way."

Fable sat in silence, absorbing Sage's words. The fox realized that the journey had indeed been the source of profound wisdom and growth. Fable no longer desired to reach the fountain but to continue exploring and learning from the world around him.

From that day forward, Fable and Sage travelled together, sharing their stories and knowledge with others. Fable's heart was filled with contentment, knowing that the journey of wisdom was never-ending and that each step brought new understanding.

And so, they lived their days, not seeking a final destination, but embracing the endless journey of life, where every moment was an opportunity to learn and grow.

The story teaches us that the pursuit of wisdom and fulfilment is a continuous journey. True contentment comes not from reaching a final goal but from appreciating and learning from the experiences along the way.

One of our biggest challenges is ensuring that our ambitions don't become an ever-filling nest, a relentless cycle of seeking the next comfortable thing. That's a losing proposition. Acquiring more and more can spike our satisfaction—for a moment. Then it goes back down. Over the ages, our greatest minds have pondered fulfillment, and their conclusions are much the same: Continuous accumulation won't automatically lead to lasting happiness.

Using Maslow's Hierarchy of Needs, let's explore how the behaviours exemplified in the story of Fable the Fox and Sage the Tortoise can lead to an extraordinary life worth living.

Physiological Needs

In the animal world, basic needs include access to essential resources like food and shelter that support life. However, as Fable learned, the endless pursuit of material goods (like the Everlasting Fountain of Wisdom) cannot satisfy our needs if we are insatiable. By appreciating the journey and the simple beauty around us, we find fulfillment in what we have, rather than constantly seeking more.

Safety Needs

Once basic needs are met, we seek security in our environments. We want our habitats to be safe from predators and harsh conditions. Fable's journey with Sage taught him that true safety and security come not from hoarding resources but from understanding and adapting to our surroundings. Learning and growing from experiences provide a deeper sense of security than any material accumulation can.

Love and Belonging

Social connections in the animal kingdom, like packs, flocks and herds, give us a sense of belonging. Through his journey, Fable formed a meaningful bond with Sage, illustrating that genuine relationships are built on shared experiences and mutual understanding. These bonds provide a sense of belonging and emotional support that far surpasses superficial connections.

Esteem Needs

Achieving recognition in the animal hierarchy and gaining status can boost our self-esteem temporarily. However, as Fable realized, true self-esteem comes from within and is nurtured through personal growth and self-awareness. The respect and wisdom he gained from his journey with Sage were far more valuable and enduring than any external validation.

Self-Actualization

The ultimate goal is to realize our full potential. Fable's journey illustrates that true self-actualization involves continuous personal growth, creativity, and finding deeper meaning in life. The journey itself, with its lessons and experiences, was the path to self-actualization. Fable discovered that fulfillment comes not from reaching a final destination but from embracing the journey and the growth it brings.

Proving the Behaviours Lead to an Extraordinary Life

1. **Appreciation and Contentment**: Fable's shift from desiring the Everlasting Fountain of Wisdom to appreciating the journey reflects a fundamental change in mindset. This appreciation for the present and contentment with what one has leads to a more fulfilling and less stressful life.
2. **Adaptability and Growth**: By learning from Sage and the experiences along the journey, Fable became more adaptable and wiser. This growth mindset is essential for overcoming challenges and achieving long-term success and happiness.
3. **Meaningful Relationships**: The bond between Fable and Sage highlights the importance of meaningful relationships built on trust and shared experiences. These relationships provide emotional support and contribute significantly to overall well-being and happiness.

4. **Intrinsic Self-Esteem**: Fable's internal growth and self-awareness led to a more stable and enduring sense of self-esteem. This intrinsic self-esteem is less vulnerable to external circumstances and contributes to a more resilient and confident individual.
5. **Continuous Personal Development**: Embracing the journey of life as an opportunity for continuous learning and personal development leads to a richer, more meaningful existence. This pursuit of self-actualization ensures that life is dynamic, engaging, and deeply rewarding.

One of the hardest things for us is keeping our quest for knowledge from turning into an endless chase for the next bit of information that will make us feel smarter. This is not a good idea. When we collect data and facts, we often do it for the satisfaction they provide. In some ways, this does work. Gaining a better understanding of something or learning something new can spark our curiosity for a short time. But then, it fades. Great minds have long pondered education, and they've all concluded that having information and knowledge won't automatically make you enlightened.

How events affect us depends on how we interpret them in the context of our lives. If we don't see the "big picture," it's easy to get stuck in a cycle of wanting more information. Why? Because the sense of enlightenment we get from acquiring new knowledge is fleeting; we quickly get used to it. This happens to everyone, and it eventually leaves us feeling bored, prompting us to seek something new to learn or discover. Worse, we might not even pause to reflect on what we've learned because we are already chasing the next thing. If we're not careful, we wind up bouncing between learning and acquiring without ever fully enjoying any of it. This is a surefire way to stay ignorant, and the day we understand this is the day our lives change for good. So how do we find wisdom that lasts?

Consider the example of a tech enthusiast who constantly upgrades to the latest gadgets. Initially, each new device brings excitement and a sense of satisfaction. But soon after, the novelty wears off, and the search for the next upgrade begins. This cycle can keep them from truly appreciating and mastering the technology they already have.

Another example is an avid reader who buys book after book, hoping each one will bring a deeper understanding or a new perspective. They might speed through each book, driven by the thrill of acquiring knowledge. However, without taking the time to reflect on and digest the material, the insights gained are often shallow and transient.

To find lasting wisdom, we must recognize the impermanence of our desires and understand that true enlightenment comes from a deeper engagement with what we already know. This means taking the time to reflect, practise and integrate new knowledge into our lives, rather than constantly seeking the next intellectual high. Wisdom grows not from the quantity of information we acquire but from the quality of our understanding and the depth of our insights.

From the Philosophy of Albert Camus: The Pursuit of Meaning in Absurdity

Albert Camus, the renowned existential philosopher, believed that life's inherent meaninglessness, or absurdity, can lead us to a deeper understanding of happiness and fulfillment. According to Camus, we must confront the absurdity of life and embrace it to find true meaning. This engagement with the absurd is crucial for a meaningful existence.

Prioritizing Quality of Life for Extraordinary Results

One important rule for achieving great success in life is to focus on the quality of life first. This method not only gives you power but also makes you more determined and strong-willed. Knowing what makes your life better and always acting in a way that supports this knowledge is the key to success.

Focusing on making your life better will lead to understanding and conviction on its own. This clarity speeds up the process of making decisions, letting you make choices quickly and often seize the best chances. If you have the best options, you can have the most fulfilling experiences that life has to give.

Prioritizing Quality of Life for Extraordinary Results: The Story of Jan Koum

Early Struggles and Humble Beginnings

Jan Koum, the co-founder of WhatsApp, was born in a small village on the outskirts of Kyiv, Ukraine. Growing up during a time of political instability and economic hardship, Koum's family faced numerous challenges. At the age of 16, he immigrated to the United States with his mother and grandmother, seeking a better life. They settled in Mountain View, California, where they relied on welfare support to make ends meet.

Koum's mother worked as a babysitter, and he himself took up odd jobs to contribute to the household income. Despite their struggles, Koum was determined to improve their situation through education and hard work.

Prioritizing Education and Skill Development

Koum enrolled in San Jose State University while simultaneously working as a security tester at Ernst & Young. It was during this time that he developed a deep interest in programming and networking. Recognizing the importance of quality education, he prioritized his studies and continuously honed his technical skills.

In 1997, Koum joined Yahoo as an infrastructure engineer. For the next nine years, he immersed himself in the tech industry, gaining valuable experience and learning from some of the best minds in the field. Despite the demanding nature of his job, Koum never lost sight of his ultimate goal—to create something impactful that would improve people's lives.

The Birth of WhatsApp

In 2009, Koum, along with his friend Brian Acton, founded WhatsApp Inc. The inspiration behind WhatsApp was simple—to create a messaging app that prioritized user experience and privacy. Koum was adamant about not compromising on quality, and he ensured that the app was free of advertisements and maintained strong encryption to protect users' data.

Koum's commitment to quality of life extended beyond the app's features. He fostered a work environment that valued employee well-being, emphasizing a healthy work–life balance and encouraging innovation. This focus on quality and user-centric design quickly propelled WhatsApp to global popularity.

Extraordinary Success and Legacy

In 2014, Facebook acquired WhatsApp for a staggering $19 billion, making it one of the largest tech acquisitions in history. Koum's journey from a struggling immigrant to a billionaire entrepreneur is a testament to the power of prioritizing quality of life.

By focusing on education and skill development, and creating a product that genuinely improved people's lives, Koum achieved extraordinary results. His story serves as an inspiration for aspiring entrepreneurs and professionals, highlighting that prioritizing quality of life, both personally and for others, can lead to unprecedented success.

Jan Koum's rags-to-riches story underscores the importance of prioritizing quality of life for extraordinary results. From his early struggles to his monumental success, Koum's journey is a shining example of how focusing on what truly matters can lead to remarkable achievements.

That being said, life isn't always easy. Problems and difficulties will always be there. These are the times when a good life really shows how valuable it is. Knowing what makes your life better gives you the drive and energy to get through hard times. To get amazing results, you need to be able to keep your promises for long enough to see them through.

Making a promise to improve your quality of life will keep you focused on your goals. Everything goes smoothly when your actions are in line with your desire to live a good life. Your daily habits are in line with your beliefs, which gives you a sense of rhythm and balance. This alignment can even make you feel happy in the most surprising ways, like when you start to hum or whistle as you go about your day.

To sum up, focusing on quality of life isn't just about making better decisions; it's also about making your life feel like it fits with your core values and goals. This way of thinking turns problems into chances and normal activities into steps towards a better, more satisfying life.

14

Celebrate Your Life

My mission in life is not merely to survive, but to thrive; and to do so with some passion, some compassion, some humour and some style.

—Maya Angelou

Life is a magnificent journey filled with moments of joy, challenges, growth, and endless possibilities. To celebrate life means to embrace every aspect of it, from the mundane to the extraordinary. By embracing the present, celebrating your journey, staying curious, living with intention, spreading joy and kindness, and cultivating gratitude, you can create a life that is not only fulfilling but also deeply enriching. Let's delve into these concepts with real-life examples and the theory of gratitude.

Embrace the Present: Find Joy in the Here and Now

The present moment is all we truly have. By focusing on the now, you can unlock a sense of peace and contentment that often eludes those who dwell too much on the past or worry excessively about the future.

Example: Mindfulness in Daily Life

Consider the practice of mindfulness, which has been shown to reduce stress and increase happiness. Take Sarah, for instance, a busy professional who used to feel overwhelmed by her hectic schedule. By incorporating mindfulness into her daily routine, such as taking a few minutes each morning to meditate and being fully present during her meals, Sarah began to notice the small joys of life. She felt the warmth of the sun during her morning walk, enjoyed the taste of her food, and appreciated her interactions with colleagues. This shift in focus allowed her to find joy in the present moment and significantly improved her overall well-being.

Celebrate Your Journey: Honour Your Progress

Every step you take in life, no matter how small, is a part of your journey. Celebrating your progress helps you recognize your achievements and motivates you to continue moving forward.

Example: Personal Growth and Achievements

Imagine John, who struggled with self-doubt and low self-esteem. Over the years, he worked hard to develop his skills and advance in his career. By keeping a journal where he noted his achievements and reflected on his growth, John could see how far he had come. Celebrating milestones such as completing a challenging project or receiving positive feedback from his boss helped him appreciate his efforts and built his confidence.

Stay Curious and Open: Embrace Life's Surprises

Curiosity keeps life exciting and opens the door to new experiences and learning opportunities. It encourages you to explore the world with a sense of wonder and eagerness.

Example: Lifelong Learning

Take the story of Maria, a retired teacher who always had a passion for painting but never pursued it. After retirement, she decided to take art classes. Her curiosity and openness to learning something new brought immense joy and fulfillment. Maria not only discovered a hidden talent but also made new friends and felt a renewed sense of purpose. Her willingness to stay curious allowed her to embrace new opportunities and experiences.

Live with Intention: Guided by Your Values and Aspirations

Living with intention means aligning your actions with your core values and long-term goals. It involves making conscious choices that reflect what truly matters to you.

Example: Purposeful Living

Consider David, who realized that his high-paying job in the corporate world did not align with his passion for helping others. He decided to transition into a career in social work. Although it meant a pay cut, David found immense satisfaction in his work. By living with intention and making choices based on his values, he felt more fulfilled and connected to his purpose.

Spread Joy and Kindness: Uplift Others

Kindness and joy influence both giver and recipient deeply. Kindness starts a chain reaction that improves the mood and bonds people.

Example: The Ripple Effect of Kindness

Emily, a young woman working at a café, decided to start a "pay it forward" chain by buying a coffee for the next customer in line. This small act of kindness inspired others to do the same, creating a wave of goodwill that brightened the day of many customers. Emily's simple gesture not only uplifted those around her but also brought her a deep sense of happiness and connection.

Cultivate Gratitude: The Theory of Gratitude

Gratitude is a powerful practice that can transform your perspective on life. It involves recognizing and appreciating the positive aspects of your life, no matter how small.

Theory of Gratitude: Gratitude has been extensively studied in positive psychology and is considered a key component of well-being. Researchers like Robert Emmons have shown that practising gratitude can lead to increased happiness, better physical health, improved relationships and greater resilience. When you focus on what you're grateful for, you shift your mindset from one of scarcity to one of abundance.

Example: Gratitude Journaling

Lisa, a college student, felt overwhelmed by the pressures of academic life. She started a gratitude journal, writing down three things she was grateful for each day. This practice helped her focus on the positive aspects of her life, such as supportive friends, good health and the opportunity to learn. Over time, Lisa noticed a significant improvement in her mood and overall outlook on life.

Embrace, Celebrate, Stay Curious, Live with Intention, Spread Joy, and Cultivate Gratitude

Practical Tips to Implement These Principles:

1. **Mindfulness Practice:** Dedicate a few minutes each day to mindfulness meditation. Focus on your breath and the sensations around you to ground yourself in the present moment.
2. **Celebrate Small Wins:** Keep a journal of your achievements, no matter how small. Reflect on your progress regularly to stay motivated and appreciate your journey.
3. **Stay Curious:** Make a list of things you've always wanted to learn or try. Set aside time each week to explore these interests, whether it's reading a book, taking a class or visiting a new place.
4. **Live Intentionally:** Identify your core values and goals. Make decisions that align with these values, and set clear, actionable steps to achieve your aspirations.
5. **Spread Joy:** Perform random acts of kindness. This could be as simple as complimenting a stranger, helping a neighbour, or volunteering your time for a good cause.
6. **Gratitude Practice:** Start a gratitude journal. Each day, write down three things you're grateful for. Reflect on these entries regularly to cultivate a positive mindset.

Boosting dopamine levels can enhance mood, motivation, and overall well-being, making it easier to celebrate life. Here are some short exercises that can help increase dopamine and add joy to your daily routine. These exercises are simple and effective, and can be integrated into your day without requiring significant time or effort.

1. Physical Exercise: Quick Workouts

Aerobic Exercise (10–15 minutes)

- **Jumping Jacks:** Do two sets of 30 seconds each with a 15-second rest in between. This increases heart rate and dopamine release.
- **High Knees:** Run in place for one minute, lifting your knees as high as possible. Repeat twice with a 30-second break.
- **Dancing:** Put on your favorite song and dance like nobody's watching. Dancing is a fun way to increase dopamine and celebrate your life.

Strength Training (10 minutes)

- **Bodyweight Squats:** Do three sets of 15 squats. Squats engage large muscle groups, which can boost dopamine.
- **Push-ups:** Perform three sets of 10 push-ups. Modify by doing them on your knees if needed.
- **Plank:** Hold a plank position for 30 seconds. Rest for 15 seconds and repeat twice.

2. Mindfulness and Meditation: Mental Clarity

Meditation (5–10 minutes)

- **Mindful Breathing:** Sit comfortably, close your eyes, and focus on your breath. Inhale deeply for a count of four,

hold for four, and exhale for four. Repeat for 5–10 minutes. This calms the mind and increases dopamine levels.
- **Body Scan:** Lie down and mentally scan your body from head to toe, noticing any areas of tension. This exercise promotes relaxation and dopamine release.

3. Gratitude Practice: Emotional Well-Being

Gratitude Journaling (5 minutes)

- **Daily Gratitude List:** Write down three things you are grateful for each day. Reflecting on positive aspects of your life boosts dopamine and overall happiness.
- **Gratitude Letter:** Write a letter to someone you appreciate. Expressing gratitude strengthens relationships and increases dopamine.

4. Creativity and Hobbies: Personal Fulfillment

Artistic Expression (10–15 minutes)

- **Drawing or Doodling:** Spend a few minutes drawing or doodling. Engaging in creative activities stimulates dopamine production.
- **Playing a Musical Instrument:** Play an instrument you enjoy for 10–15 minutes. Music can significantly boost dopamine and mood.

Learning and Curiosity (10 minutes)

- **Reading:** Read a chapter of a book or an article on a topic that interests you. Learning new things enhances dopamine levels.
- **Puzzles and Games:** Solve a puzzle or play a brain game. These activities challenge the mind and increase dopamine.

5. Social Interaction: Strengthening Connections

Connecting with Others (5–10 minutes)

- **Phone Call or Video Chat:** Call or video chat with a friend or family member. Positive social interactions boost dopamine.
- **Compliment Someone:** Give a sincere compliment to someone. Acts of kindness and positive interactions increase dopamine for both the giver and receiver.

6. Nature and Outdoor Activities: Refreshing the Mind

Outdoor Activities (10–15 minutes)

- **Nature Walk:** Take a brisk walk in a park or natural setting. Being in nature and getting sunlight enhances dopamine production.
- **Gardening:** Spend a few minutes tending to a garden or indoor plants. This can be relaxing and rewarding, boosting dopamine.

Detailed Routine for a Dopamine-Boosting Day

Morning:

1. **Mindful Breathing:** Five minutes to start the day calmly.
2. **Jumping Jacks and High Knees:** 10 minutes to energize and boost dopamine.

Mid-Morning:

1. **Gratitude Journaling:** Five minutes to list three things you are grateful for.

Afternoon:

1. **Drawing or Doodling:** 10 minutes to engage creativity.

2. **Bodyweight Squats and Push-ups:** 10 minutes for a physical boost.

Evening:

1. **Nature Walk:** 15 minutes in a park to refresh your mind.
2. **Phone Call:** 10 minutes connecting with a friend or family member.

Night:

1. **Gratitude Letter:** Write a short letter to someone you appreciate.
2. **Mindful Breathing:** Five minutes before bed to relax and reflect on the day.

Golden Nuggets

1. Embrace the Present: Live Mindfully

Takeaway: Focus on the present moment to find peace and contentment. Mindfulness can significantly enhance your well-being by allowing you to fully experience and appreciate the small joys of daily life.

Example: Embrace mindfulness by weaving meditation into your daily routine. Take a few moments each morning to meditate or immerse yourself fully in the present during meals. This simple practice can melt away stress and elevate your happiness.

2. Celebrate Your Journey: Recognize and Honour Your Progress

Takeaway: Every step in your journey, no matter how small, is worth celebrating. Recognizing your progress boosts motivation and confidence, helping you move forward with a positive outlook.

Example: Keep a journal to note your achievements and milestones. Reflecting on these moments helps you appreciate your efforts and growth, as seen in the example of John who documented his personal and professional achievements.

3. Stay Curious and Open: Embrace New Experiences

Takeaway: Curiosity keeps life exciting and leads to continuous learning and personal growth. Embracing new experiences with an open mind can bring joy and fulfillment.

Example: Pursue new interests or hobbies, like Maria who took art classes after retirement. This not only brought her joy but also introduced her to new friends and opportunities.

15

Nothing Doing

Time you enjoy wasting is not wasted time.

—Bertrand Russell

The Procrastinator's Reverie: An Exegesis

In the lineage of Scandinavian well-being philosophies, first came hygge, the Danish embrace of cosy domesticity, followed by lagom, the Swedish balance of moderation. Now, emerging from the Netherlands, we encounter Niksen: An invitation to the profound art of doing nothing, a concept that resists the tyranny of productivity and the hegemony of purpose.

What Is Niksen?

In its etymological purity, Niksen represents the act of doing nothing, of embracing idleness without the teleological drive towards productivity. Carolien Hamming, steward of the CSR Centrum, elucidates Niksen as the act of existing without intent, an ontological state of pure being, akin to what Heidegger might consider *gelassenheit*. To practise Niksen is to engage in acts devoid of utility—sitting, observing or simply listening—not as a means to an end, but as ends in themselves.

Dr Emily Thompson, an expert in existential psychology, argues that while mindfulness demands presence and focus, Niksen allows the mind to traverse a liminal space of unrestrained thought. It is a departure from cognitive-behavioural frameworks, embracing instead an existential acceptance of being. Niksen eschews productivity and goal-orientation, offering instead a pure engagement with the experience of *being-in-the-world* in its most authentic form.

The Benefits of Niksen

Historically dismissed as mere sloth, Niksen now finds re-evaluation within the context of escalating global stress. Eve Ekman of the Greater Good Science Center posits Niksen as a bulwark against the existential dread of modernity. Stress, that pernicious agent of our age, finds its antithesis in Niksen—a space where anxiety dissipates and the body rejuvenates. Niksen, therefore, becomes a praxis of resistance, a subversion of the capitalist ethos of ceaseless production.

Practising Niksen

Yet, the praxis of Niksen is not without its paradoxes. The inertia of inactivity can be discomfiting, particularly for those habituated to the frenetic cadence of contemporary life. Hamming acknowledges this disquiet, advocating a gradual acclimatization to idleness. The act of *daring to be idle* demands a reclamation of temporality, a reorientation of the self within the flux of existence.

The Downsides of Niksen

However, like all dialectics, Niksen harbours potential negatives. The wandering mind, unfettered, may descend into rumination, a maelstrom of recursive thought. Ekman warns of the physiological repercussions of unbridled mental drift—heightened heart rates and disrupted sleep cycles. Yet, these transient effects do not eclipse the long-term benefits, wherein daydreaming, especially of intimate connections, correlates with enhanced life satisfaction.

Striking a Balance

Niksen cannot dominate the entirety of existence; it must be harmonized with active engagement. Veenhoven emphasizes the necessity of balance—productive endeavours imbue life with social connectivity and self-efficacy, fostering a cyclical relationship between happiness and productivity. The equilibrium of idleness and activity engenders a holistic well-being.

Production Procrastination: A New Perspective

From this ontological framework of Niksen, we derive a novel paradigm: productive procrastination. In a world obsessed with productivity, this concept invites us to consider strategic idleness as a conduit for creativity.

The Art of Intentional Procrastination

Imagine yourself besieged by tasks, deadlines looming like Kafkaesque specters. Instead of yielding to the compulsion to persevere, grant yourself the liberty to pause. This is not indolence but tactical respite, a Barthesian *jouissance* within the interstices of labour.

Poetic Procrastination

In the interlude of tasks undone,
Lies the elegy of none. Pause, breathe,
Let your mind unfurl,
In the void, ideas swirl.

Quotable Wisdom

> *Procrastination is not the nemesis of productivity;*
> *it is the midwife of creativity.*
>
> —Anonymous Sage

Conversation with a Mentor

You: I am engulfed by my workload. Should I not persevere?
Mentor: Sometimes, retreating into intentional procrastination cultivates greater clarity and innovation.
You: But is this not a squandering of time?
Mentor: To the contrary, it enhances the efficacy of your labour. Consider it as recharging the cognitive faculties.

Steps to Embrace Productive Procrastination

1. **Identify Moments for Pause**: Recognize when your productivity ebbs. These are opportune moments for a strategic pause.
2. **Set Boundaries**: Allocate definitive times for these interludes to prevent protracted inactivity.
3. **Engage in Low-Effort Activities**: During these intervals, partake in activities demanding minimal cognitive engagement—doodling, walking or listening to music.
4. **Reflect and Refocus**: Post-pause, contemplate any emergent ideas or perspectives. Harness this rejuvenated state to address tasks with renewed vigour.

A Procrastinator's Manifesto

Embrace the art of idleness. Relinquish guilt and permit yourself to recharge. Balance life with mindful repose and focused action. Celebrate minor victories and indulge in laughter.

Practical Application

Incorporating productive procrastination can revolutionize your approach to work and leisure. Consider these practical implementations:

- **Morning Rituals**: Commence your day with intentional idleness—quiet reflection with a cup of tea, allowing thoughts to flow unimpeded.
- **Midday Breaks**: Schedule a brief interlude in your workday to disengage from tasks. Engage in enjoyable, effortless activities.
- **Evening Wind-Down**: Conclude your day with reflective idleness—watching the sunset, journaling, or silent contemplation.

The Science Behind It

Empirical research corroborates that interspersed breaks augment creativity and problem-solving. A mind unshackled by constant focus can uncover novel insights and solutions. Studies indicate that downtime facilitates more effective information processing, enhancing outcomes in both personal and professional realms.

Balancing Activity and Rest

The fulcrum of well-being lies in balancing activity with rest. Productivity is essential, yet the permission to do nothing is equally vital. This balance fosters a sustainable and gratifying approach to life and labour.

Embracing the art of doing nothing through productive procrastination unveils a new dimension of equilibrium and joy. Permit yourself the luxury of idleness, recharging, and allowing your mind to wander. Return to your endeavours with a refreshed perspective and renewed energy. Indulge in moments of idleness—you have earned them.

Finding Balance in the Chaos

Life is a juggling act, and finding balance is key. Here are some practical tips to help you integrate mindfulness, prayer and productive procrastination into your daily routine:

The Sweetness of Doing Nothing

In our journey to understand human experience, we encounter the enchanting Italian concept of **La Dolce Far Niente**, which translates to "the sweetness of doing nothing." This idea is not merely about idleness but represents a deeper existential engagement with life. Popularized in modern culture by Elizabeth Gilbert's *Eat, Pray, Love*, La Dolce Far Niente invites us to savour life's simple pleasures without the constant drive for productivity.

Cultural Context of La Dolce Far Niente

In a scene from Gilbert's book, set in a Roman barbershop, the protagonist learns about La Dolce Far Niente amidst the warmth of Italian culture. The characters in this scene enjoy the simple pleasure of just being, indulging in desserts and conversation. This scene sharply contrasts with American culture, where relaxation often means passive consumption—like lying on a couch, drinking beer, and watching TV.

In Italy, people embrace spontaneous leisure. A man might come home from work, take a nap, feel the urge to visit a café, or spend intimate time with his partner. This narrative, while perhaps idealized, encourages us to rethink our devotion to routine and constant activity.

Philosophical Insights on Idleness

Philosopher Immanuel Kant might see La Dolce Far Niente as a fundamental condition for experiencing the sublime in everyday life. It goes against the idea that we must always act towards a specific goal, instead valuing a state of purposeless being. This idleness is not mere inactivity but a reflective state that lets the self emerge beyond practical reasoning.

Henry David Thoreau's reflections in *Walden* align with this idea. When he talks about wandering without a set direction, he embodies the Kantian concept of freedom as autonomy from external pressures. In such moments, instinct rather than routine guides action, leading to a fuller engagement with existence.

Practical Ways to Embrace La Dolce Far Niente

Imagine incorporating La Dolce Far Niente into your daily routine. Instead of giving in to the constant demands of modern life—checking emails, updating social media, or binge-watching shows—what if you created periods of intentional idleness? This would require resisting the ingrained work ethic that glorifies constant activity.

Picture the change: Instead of saving leisure for rare vacations, you could sprinkle moments of dolce far niente throughout each day. Simple acts like reading, meditating or just staring out the window could become profound engagements with the present moment.

Psychological and Existential Benefits

Psychologically, unstructured time can foster creativity and problem-solving. Cognitive science shows that when the brain is free from constant stimulation, it enters a default mode that allows for introspection and daydreaming, leading to insights and emotional regulation.

Existentially, embracing La Dolce Far Niente challenges the modern obsession with busyness. It affirms life's inherent value, independent of productivity. By cultivating these moments, we honour our existence and reclaim our autonomy from the demands of efficiency.

Detailed Steps to Integrate La Dolce Far Niente into Daily Life

Savouring the Present Moment

The sweetness of doing nothing is ultimately about being present. It allows us to deeply appreciate life as it happens, without the pressure of past regrets or future worries. This practice is a form of gratitude, recognizing the inherent worth of our lived experience.

1. **Set the Intentions:** Start your day with a clear intention. This simple practice can profoundly affect your mindset and actions throughout the day. Your intention might be, "Today, I will be present in everything I do." This creates a mental framework that prioritizes mindfulness over productivity, helping you to focus on being rather than doing.
2. **Create Your Rituals:** Develop small rituals that bring mindfulness and spirituality into your daily life. These rituals don't need to be elaborate; they can be as simple as a morning meditation, a midday gratitude break, or an evening reflection. For instance, starting your day with a few minutes of meditation can centre your mind and prepare you for the day ahead. A midday gratitude break can help you pause and appreciate the small things in life, reinforcing the practice of mindfulness. An evening

reflection can provide a moment to unwind and review your day, fostering a sense of closure and peace.
3. **Embrace Your Imperfection:** Remember, it's okay to have off days. Don't beat yourself up if you don't stick to your routines perfectly. The goal is progress, not perfection. Embracing imperfection means understanding that life is inherently unpredictable, and it's okay to deviate from your plans. This mindset can reduce stress and help you approach life with more flexibility and resilience.
4. **Celebrate ALL Wins:** Acknowledge and celebrate your small achievements. Whether it's completing a task or taking a mindful moment, every step counts. Celebrating small wins can boost your motivation and reinforce positive behaviours. It's about recognizing that even the smallest accomplishments contribute to your overall well-being and progress.
5. **Laugh ALWAYS:** Humour is a powerful tool for maintaining balance. Find joy in the little things, and don't take life too seriously. Laughter can reduce stress, improve your mood, and foster a sense of connection with others. Incorporate humour into your daily life by watching a funny video, sharing a joke with a friend, or simply finding humour in everyday situations.

Productive Procrastination

Productive procrastination is the idea of engaging in tasks that are not the primary focus but still add value in some way. This concept can be intertwined with La Dolce Far Niente to create a balanced approach to work and leisure.

6. **Engage in Creative Hobbies:** Creative hobbies like painting, writing or playing music can serve as a form of productive procrastination. These activities allow you to relax and

recharge while still engaging your mind in a meaningful way. They provide a break from your main tasks and can spark new ideas and inspiration.
7. **Learn Something New Always:** Using downtime to learn something new, whether it's a language, a skill or a topic of interest, can be a productive form of procrastination. This not only enriches your knowledge but also provides a sense of accomplishment and progress.
8. **Organize Your Space:** Organizing your physical space can be a productive way to procrastinate. It creates a more conducive environment for focus and can be a meditative practice in itself. Decluttering your workspace or rearranging your living area can provide a sense of order and clarity.

The Art of Doing Nothing: Mastering the Balance

Mastering the art of doing nothing involves finding a balance between activity and rest. It's about creating a lifestyle that values moments of stillness as much as moments of action.

9. **Practice Mindful Breathing:** Mindful breathing is a simple yet effective way to embrace La Dolce Far Niente. Taking a few deep breaths can help you centre yourself and become more present. It's a quick practise that can be done anywhere, anytime, to bring a sense of calm and clarity.
10. **Enjoy Nature Around You:** Spending time in nature is a wonderful way to practise the art of doing nothing. Whether it's a walk in the park, a hike in the mountains, or simply sitting by a lake, nature can help you disconnect from the hustle and bustle of daily life and reconnect with your inner self.
11. **Disconnect from Technology:** Technology often keeps us in a constant state of activity. By intentionally disconnecting

from your devices for a while, you can create space for La Dolce Far Niente. Use this time to engage in activities that don't require screens, like reading a book, journalling, or simply daydreaming.

Combining Productivity and Procrastination

The key to integrating La Dolce Far Niente and productive procrastination is balance. By intentionally incorporating periods of idleness and mindful activities into your day, you can enhance your overall well-being and productivity.

12. **Schedule Downtime:** Just as you schedule work tasks, schedule downtime in your calendar. This ensures that you make time for rest and relaxation, which are essential for maintaining a healthy work–life balance. Treat these periods with the same importance as your work commitments.
13. **Reflect and Adjust:** Regularly reflect on your balance of activity and rest. Are you giving yourself enough time to relax and recharge? Are you finding joy in both your productive and idle moments? Adjust your routine as needed to ensure you're nurturing both your mind and body.

Embracing a Fuller Way of Living

Integrating La Dolce Far Niente into our lives can transform how we relate to time and activity. It encourages us to find beauty in stillness, savour the present moment, and realize that the essence of life lies not in doing, but in being. By embracing the art of doing nothing and productive procrastination, we can discover a richer, more fulfilling way of living that honours both our need for productivity and our need for rest.

By accepting the art of eating, praying and even procrastinating mindfully, you'll discover a new level of balance and joy in your life. So go ahead, indulge in that extra slice of pizza, say a little prayer, and take a well-deserved break. You've earned it!

Turning Delays into Delights

Short-Term Mood Lifters

Let's take a trip back to the early 2000s, when researchers at Case Western Reserve University in Ohio made a groundbreaking discovery: Procrastination can be a mood lifter! Imagine this scenario: Participants read some really sad stories (cue the sad violin music), and as expected, their moods took a nosedive. But instead of diving into their assigned tasks, they chose to do puzzles and play video games. Why? Because these activities brought them joy, a quick fix to shake off those blues.

Further studies supported this notion: a low mood triggers procrastination only if there are fun distractions available and if people believe they can change their mood. In one particularly amusing study, researchers used "mood-freezing candles" to trick some participants into thinking their bad mood was fixed. The result? They didn't bother procrastinating since they thought their mood couldn't improve anyway. This highlights that procrastination is essentially an emotional regulation strategy, a quick switch to happy mode.

The Hedonic Shift: Procrastination's Secret Weapon

Channelling our inner Jean-Paul Sartre, let's philosophize a bit. Procrastination isn't about being lazy or bad at time management. It's about prioritizing our emotional well-being. When faced with tasks that feel like a drag, we naturally gravitate towards activities that promise instant joy. Sartre might say that in confronting the "nausea" of our daily tasks, we seek distractions that affirm our existence in fleeting moments of joy.

The Dopamine Delight: A Happiness Hack

Now, let's geek out on the science of happiness. When we procrastinate, our brains reward us with a delightful rush of dopamine, the neurotransmitter that makes us feel good. Different types of dopamine surges occur when we indulge in enjoyable distractions:

1. **Anticipation Dopamine**: This is the rush we get just by thinking about the fun activity. Imagining watching a cat video can already make us feel better.
2. **Reward Dopamine**: This kicks in when we actually engage in the activity. Watching that hilarious cat video? Boom! Instant dopamine delight.
3. **Reflection Dopamine**: This is the afterglow, the joy we feel when reminiscing about the fun activity.

These dopamine hits create a cycle of short-term happiness, reinforcing our procrastination habits. It's our brain's sneaky way of seeking a quick happiness boost amid the monotony of less enjoyable tasks.

Procrastination: A Catalyst for Success

Wait, what? Procrastination can lead to success? You bet! Here's how:

1. **Creative Incubation**: By delaying a task, our subconscious mind continues to work on it. This can lead to sudden insights or creative breakthroughs. Think of it as letting your brain marinate in creative juices.
2. **Stress Relief**: Taking breaks to engage in enjoyable activities can reduce overall stress, making us more focused and productive when we return to our tasks. It's like a mini-vacation for your brain.

3. **Motivation Boost**: Sometimes, the pressure of a looming deadline can enhance our performance. This adrenaline rush can lead to higher efficiency and better results. It's the thrill of the last-minute sprint!

The Sartrean Perspective on Happiness and Success

Sartre's existential philosophy emphasizes the importance of freedom and choice in defining our essence. Procrastination, seen through this lens, is a choice that asserts our freedom to seek happiness. It's an act of rebellion against the tyranny of productivity. By choosing joy in the moment, we exercise our existential freedom, affirming our right to be happy.

Making Procrastination Productive: Tips and Tricks

Okay, so how can we turn this procrastination habit into something productive? Here are some fun and practical suggestions:

1. **Procrastinate with Purpose**: Engage in activities that are still productive in some way. Instead of mindlessly scrolling through social media, why not read an interesting article, listen to an educational podcast, or watch a documentary?
2. **Creative Breaks**: Use your procrastination time to indulge in creative pursuits. Draw, paint, write a short story, or brainstorm ideas for a project. Creativity can be a fantastic way to procrastinate productively.
3. **Learning New Skills**: Pick up a new skill during your procrastination breaks. Learn a new language, try coding, or even pick up a musical instrument. This way, you're still enriching your life even while avoiding your main tasks.
4. **Organize and Declutter**: Procrastinate by tidying up your workspace or organizing your files. A clean and organized

environment can boost your productivity when you finally get back to work.
5. **Exercise**: Take a break to move your body. Do some yoga, go for a run, or have a dance party in your living room. Exercise can boost your mood and energy levels, making you more effective when you return to your tasks.
6. **Mindfulness and Meditation**: Use procrastination time to practise mindfulness or meditation. It can help reduce stress and improve your focus. Plus, it's a great way to hit the reset button on your brain.
7. **Networking and Socializing**: Connect with colleagues, friends or family. Networking can open up new opportunities and ideas, while socializing can provide emotional support and a sense of community.

Balancing Procrastination with Long-Term Goals

While procrastination can bring short-term joy, we also need to keep an eye on our long-term goals. Here's how to balance both:

1. **Embrace Psychological Flexibility**: Learn to tolerate uncomfortable thoughts and feelings. Stay present and focus on actions that align with your values.
2. **Enhance Committed Action**: Find creative ways to pursue your goals. If you value creativity, take breaks to engage in activities that inspire you.
3. **Mindfulness Practice**: Mindfulness helps increase psychological flexibility. It trains you to stay in the present moment, reducing the urge to procrastinate.

Practical Tips to Harness the Power of Procrastination

1. **Next Action Focus**: When tempted to procrastinate, ask yourself, "What's the next action I would take on this task

if I were to start now?" This shifts your focus from feelings to actionable steps.
2. **Reward Yourself**: Use enjoyable activities as rewards for completing tasks. This creates a positive feedback loop, making you more likely to stay productive.
3. **Break Tasks into Smaller Steps**: Large tasks can be overwhelming. Breaking them into smaller, manageable steps can make them less daunting, reducing the urge to procrastinate.

Procrastination is not merely a flaw but a complex, multifaceted behaviour that intertwines with our quest for happiness and success. By understanding its emotional roots and leveraging its positive aspects, we can transform procrastination from a source of guilt into a tool for joy and productivity. Sartre might agree: In embracing our freedom to procrastinate, we also embrace our freedom to find happiness, even in the mundane.

The Procrastinator's Dance Routine: A Step-by-Step Guide to Joyful Delays for Professionals

Welcome to the Ultimate Procrastinator's Dance Routine! This routine is designed to lift your spirits, give you a burst of energy, and make procrastination a productive and fun part of your day. So, put on your favourite upbeat music, and let's get moving!

Step 1: The Warm-Up Wiggle

- **Find Your Groove:** Choose a song that makes you want to move. It could be anything from disco to pop, as long as it gets you excited.
- **Shake It Out:** Stand up and shake out your arms and legs. Loosen up your body and get rid of any stiffness.

- **Head Bobbing:** Start bobbing your head to the beat of the music. Feel the rhythm and let it take over.

Step 2: The Funky Footwork

- **Step Touch:** Step to the right with your right foot, then bring your left foot to meet it. Step to the left with your left foot, and bring your right foot to meet it. Repeat this for eight counts.
- **Grapevine:** Step your right foot to the right, cross your left foot behind your right, step your right foot to the right again, and tap your left foot next to your right. Reverse the steps to the left. Do this for eight counts.
- **Heel-Toe Tap:** Tap your right heel forward, then your right toe back. Repeat with your left foot. Alternate sides for eight counts.

Step 3: The Sassy Shuffle

- **Side Shuffle:** Take three quick steps to the right and clap your hands. Take three quick steps to the left and clap your hands. Repeat for eight counts.
- **Hip Rolls:** Roll your hips in a big circle to the right for four counts, then to the left for four counts. Make those circles as big and sassy as you can!
- **Shoulder Shimmy:** Shimmy your shoulders by moving them back and forth quickly. Add some flair by moving your arms up and down as you shimmy.

Step 4: The Procrastinator's Pizzazz

- **Freestyle Fun:** Let loose and dance however you feel! Spin around, jump, do the robot—whatever makes you smile. This is your moment to shine and embrace the joy of procrastination.

- **Jazz Hands:** Finish your freestyle with some dramatic jazz hands. Spread your fingers wide and shake your hands up high for a grand finale.

Step 5: The Cool Down

- **Slow Sway:** Slow down the tempo and sway from side to side. Let your body relax and enjoy the gentle movements.
- **Stretch It Out:** Stretch your arms overhead, then bend down to touch your toes. Hold each stretch for a few seconds to release any tension.
- **Deep Breaths:** Take a few deep breaths in through your nose and out through your mouth. Feel the calm and satisfaction of a dance well done.

Procrastinator's Hobby: The Art of Fun Doodling

Step 1: Gather Your Supplies

- **Paper:** Grab a stack of blank paper or a sketchbook.
- **Pens and Pencils:** Get a variety of pens, pencils, markers, and coloured pencils. The more colours, the better!
- **Inspiration:** Find something to inspire you—a favourite quote, a picture or just your imagination.

Step 2: Set the Scene

- **Comfort Zone:** Find a comfortable spot to doodle. This could be a cosy corner of your room, a sunny spot by the window, or even at your desk.
- **Background Music:** Play some relaxing music to set the mood. Instrumental music works great, but anything that helps you focus is perfect.

Step 3: The Doodling Basics

- **Start Simple:** Begin with simple shapes like circles, squares, and triangles. Fill a whole page with these shapes to get your hand warmed up.
- **Line Magic:** Practise drawing different types of lines—straight, wavy, zigzag and spirals. Experiment with line thickness by pressing harder or softer with your pen or pencil.
- **Pattern Play:** Create patterns by repeating shapes and lines. Try making a page full of interconnected circles or a maze of zigzags.

Step 4: Let Your Imagination Run Wild

- **Character Creation:** Draw some fun characters. They can be animals, mythical creatures, or funny stick figures with exaggerated features.
- **Scene Setting:** Create a scene for your characters. Draw a magical forest, a bustling city or an underwater paradise. Let your imagination guide you.
- **Colour Explosion:** Add colour to your doodles. Use bright, bold colours or soft pastels. Don't worry about staying within the lines—this is about having fun!

Step 5: Doodle Challenges

- **30-Second Doodles:** Set a timer for 30 seconds and see what you can create in that time. The goal is to draw quickly and not worry about perfection.
- **Blindfolded Doodles:** Close your eyes or use a blindfold and try to draw something. This can lead to hilarious and unexpected results.

- **Collaborative Doodles:** If you have a friend nearby, take turns adding to a doodle. This can create some wonderfully wacky art.

Step 6: Showcase Your Art

- **Doodle Wall:** Tape your favourite doodles to a wall or a bulletin board to create an inspiring display.
- **Share Online:** Share your doodles on social media or with friends. You might inspire others to join in the fun.
- **Doodle Diary:** Keep a doodle diary where you can document your daily doodles. It's a wonderful way to track your progress and creativity over time.

Embrace the Fun

Whether you're dancing away your procrastination blues or doodling to your heart's content, remember that these activities are all about embracing joy and creativity. So next time you find yourself putting off a task, grab your dancing shoes or your doodling supplies and turn that procrastination into a celebration of fun and productivity!

16

The Life Commandments

*To be happy, we must not be
too concerned with others.*

—Albert Camus

Commandment I: Thou Shalt Balance Thy Work and Play

Work:

- **Wake Up and Smell the Coffee:** Every morning, greet the day with a cup of ambition (and a strong brew).
- **Prioritize like a Pro:** Make a to-do list that puts Marie Kondo's organization skills to shame.
- **Meetings:** Keep them short and sweet. Use PowerPoints sparingly, and always bring donuts.

Life:

- **Mindfulness:** Practise yoga, meditate or just stare at a tree for 10 minutes a day.
- **Passions:** Pursue a hobby that makes you forget you have a job. Crochet, kickboxing or birdwatching—it's all fair game.
- **Recharge:** Schedule "me-time" like it's a non-negotiable meeting with Beyoncé.

Party:

- **Prep Work:** Know your limits. Hydrate, snack and remember where you parked.
- **Groove:** Dance like no one's watching. If they are, even better—give them a show.
- **Unwind:** Have a designated chill corner for quiet moments or deep convos about the universe.

Commandment II: Thou Shalt Communicate Effectively

Work:

- **Emails:** Clear, concise, and with a subject line that actually describes the email.
- **Feedback:** Give it constructively, receive it gracefully. Sandwich method: positive, constructive, positive.
- **Meetings:** Follow the agenda. No tangents about your cat's Instagram account.

Life:

- **Relationships:** Honest and open communication is key. Avoid passive-aggressive post-it notes.
- **Conflict Resolution:** Address issues head-on. Use "I feel" statements instead of "You always" accusations.
- **Listening:** Truly listen. Don't just wait for your turn to speak.

Party:

- **Invitations:** Be clear on the when, where and what (theme, dress code, bring your own snacks?).
- **Introductions:** Make sure everyone knows everyone. Awkward silences are the enemy.
- **Goodbyes:** Don't ghost. A proper farewell, even if it's a French exit, is courteous.

Commandment III: Thou Shalt Be a Team Player

Work:

- **Collaboration:** Share the load. Two heads are better than one, unless they're arguing.
- **Credit:** Give credit where it's due. Stealing ideas is a one-way ticket to Office Drama Land.
- **Support:** Be the colleague who's always got a spare pen and a willing ear.

Life:

- **Family:** Chip in with chores. Nobody likes a couch potato (unless it's the actual food, then it's delicious).
- **Friends:** Be there. Birthdays, bad days and days ending in "y".
- **Community:** Volunteer, join a club or just be the neighbour who lends sugar without judgement.

Party:

- **Host Duties:** Make sure everyone is having a good time. Circulate, introduce and refill drinks.
- **Guest Etiquette:** RSVP, bring something (chips, flowers, yourself) and help clean up.
- **Shared Experiences:** Engage in group activities—karaoke, charades or a conga line.

Commandment IV: Thou Shalt Be Organized

Work:

- **Desk:** Tidy desk, tidy mind. Keep it clutter-free and stocked with essentials.

- **Files:** Digital and physical. Label, colour-code and back up regularly.
- **Deadlines:** Use calendars, reminders and alarms. Procrastination is a productivity killer.

Life:

- **Home:** Clean regularly. A well-kept home is a sanctuary, not a stressor.
- **Schedule:** Plan your week. Balance social, personal and professional commitments.
- **Finances:** Budget like a boss. Know where your money goes, and save for a rainy day.

Party:

- **Prep:** Plan ahead. Menu, playlist and activities sorted before guests arrive.
- **Decor:** Ambiance matters. Fairy lights, themed décor and a comfy seating area.
- **Timeline:** Have a rough schedule. Arrival, main event and a gentle nudge towards the exit.

Commandment V: Thou Shalt Keep Learning

Work:

- **Courses:** Sign up for workshops, webinars and courses. Stay ahead of the curve.
- **Mentorship:** Seek and be a mentor. Knowledge is best shared.
- **Read:** Industry news, books and articles. A well-informed mind is a powerful tool.

Life:

- **Skills:** Learn something new regularly. Cooking, a language or how to fix a leaky faucet.
- **Culture:** Visit museums, watch documentaries and attend talks.
- **Personal Growth:** Self-help books, podcasts and reflective journalling.

Party:

- **Trends:** Keep up with the latest music, dance moves and party games.
- **Cooking:** Experiment with new recipes. Impress your guests with gourmet snacks.
- **Crafts:** DIY decorations and party favors. Adds a personal touch.

Commandment VI: Thou Shalt Stay Healthy

Work:

- **Ergonomics:** Invest in a good chair, and stand up every hour.
- **Snacks:** Healthy options. Nuts, fruit and dark chocolate over chips and soda.
- **Exercise:** Desk stretches, lunchtime walks and regular breaks to move.

Life:

- **Diet:** Balanced and nutritious. Veggies, lean protein and the occasional treat.
- **Exercise:** Regular activity. Gym, yoga or dancing in your living room.

- **Mental Health:** Meditate, seek therapy if needed, and talk about your feelings.

Party:

- **Moderation:** Know your limits. Hydrate and pace yourself.
- **Safety:** Don't drink and drive. Have a plan for getting home.
- **Aftercare:** Post-party recovery plan. Hydrate, rest and have a hearty breakfast.

Commandment VII: Thou Shalt Be Respectful

Work:

- **Punctuality:** Be on time. Respect others' time as you would your own.
- **Manners:** Politeness costs nothing. Please, thank you and a smile.
- **Inclusivity:** Value diversity and create an inclusive environment.

Life:

- **Courtesy:** Hold doors, say excuse me and be kind.
- **Tolerance:** Embrace differences. Learn from others' perspectives.
- **Boundaries:** Respect personal space and boundaries. No means no.

Party:

- **Behaviour:** Be courteous. Don't be the one causing drama.
- **Space:** Respect the host's home. Don't snoop or break things.
- **Inclusivity:** Make everyone feel welcome. Avoid cliques and include new faces.

Commandment VIII: Thou Shalt Have Fun

Work:

- **Breaks:** Take them. A rested mind is a creative one.
- **Humour:** Lighten up the office with appropriate jokes and a positive attitude.
- **Celebrate:** Acknowledge milestones and achievements.

Life:

- **Adventure:** Try new things. Travel, explore and create memories.
- **Laughter:** Seek joy and laughter daily. It's good for the soul.
- **Relax:** Don't take life too seriously. Find joy in the little things.

Party:

- **Games:** Icebreakers and party games. Keep it lively and engaging.
- **Music:** A killer playlist is a must. Mix of genres to keep everyone happy.
- **Themes:** Spice things up with themed parties. Costumes, decorations and themed snacks.

Commandment IX: Thou Shalt Network

Work:

- **LinkedIn:** Keep it updated. Connect with industry peers.
- **Events:** Attend conferences, workshops and networking events.
- **Follow Up:** After meetings or events, send a follow-up email to stay connected.

Life:

- **Social Circles:** Keep in touch with friends and family. Regular catch-ups.
- **Community:** Join clubs, societies or local groups.
- **Online:** Use social media wisely. Connect with like-minded people.

Party:

- **Mixing:** Introduce people. Foster connections and new friendships.
- **Follow Up:** Send thank-you notes or messages post party.
- **Future Plans:** Plan the next get-together. Keep the momentum going.

Commandment X: Thou Shalt Be Authentic

Work:

- **Integrity:** Be honest and ethical in your dealings.
- **Authenticity:** Be yourself. Authenticity breeds trust and respect.
- **Values:** Uphold your values and principles.

Life:

- **True Self:** Embrace who you are. Don't conform to others' expectations.
- **Honesty:** Be truthful with yourself and others.
- **Passions:** Follow your passions and dreams, no matter how unconventional.

Party:

- **Genuine:** Be real. Don't put on a façade.

- **Kindness:** Treat everyone with kindness and respect.
- **Memorable:** Create genuine, lasting memories. Be present and engaged.

Commandment XI: Thou Shalt Practise Gratitude

Work:

- **Appreciation:** Thank your colleagues for their hard work and contributions.
- **Positivity:** Keep a gratitude journal at work. Write down at least one thing you're thankful for each day.
- **Recognition:** Acknowledge and celebrate team successes and milestones.

Life:

- **Daily Thanks:** Begin or end your day by listing three things you're grateful for.
- **Relationships:** Express gratitude to your loved ones regularly. A simple thank you goes a long way.
- **Mindfulness:** Appreciate the little things—a sunny day, a good book or a delicious meal.

Party:

- **Hosts:** Always thank your host. Bring a small gift or send a thank-you note afterward.
- **Guests:** Show appreciation for those who attend your party. Make them feel valued.
- **Moments:** Cherish and be grateful for the moments of joy and laughter shared.

Commandment XII: Thou Shalt Embrace Change

Work:

- **Adaptability:** Be open to new ideas and ways of doing things.
- **Learning:** Continuously seek to learn and improve. Take on new challenges.
- **Innovation:** Encourage and participate in innovative projects.

Life:

- **Flexibility:** Accept that change is a part of life. Embrace it with a positive attitude.
- **Growth:** See change as an opportunity for personal growth and development.
- **Adventures:** Seek out new experiences and adventures.

Party:

- **Spontaneity:** Be open to spontaneous party plans or changes in the agenda.
- **Trends:** Keep up with new party trends and ideas.
- **Flexibility:** Adapt to the flow of the party. Go with the vibe, even if it deviates from the plan.

Commandment XIII: Thou Shalt Foster Creativity

Work:

- **Brainstorming:** Create an environment that encourages creative thinking and problem-solving.
- **Projects:** Take on projects that challenge your creativity.
- **Workspaces:** Decorate your workspace to inspire creativity.

Life:

- **Arts:** Engage in creative activities like painting, writing or music.
- **Inspiration:** Surround yourself with inspiration. Visit art galleries, read books or watch thought-provoking movies.
- **Expression:** Find ways to express yourself creatively in everyday life.

Party:

- **Themes:** Experiment with creative themes and decorations for your parties.
- **DIY:** Make your own party favors, decorations, and snacks.
- **Activities:** Include creative activities like arts and crafts or DIY photo booths.

Commandment XIV: Thou Shalt Stay Curious

Work:

- **Questions:** Always ask questions. Seek to understand the 'why' and 'how'.
- **Exploration:** Explore different areas of your field. Don't be afraid to step out of your comfort zone.
- **Learning:** Never stop learning. Take courses, read books, and stay informed.

Life:

- **World:** Stay curious about the world. Travel, explore different cultures, and meet new people.
- **Hobbies:** Try out new hobbies and activities. Keep your mind engaged.
- **Knowledge:** Read widely and diversely. Stay informed about a variety of topics.

Party:

- **Games:** Include trivia and quiz games to spark curiosity.
- **Conversations:** Encourage interesting and engaging conversations.
- **Exploration:** Try new party venues and experiences.

Commandment XV: Thou Shalt Be Resilient

Work:

- **Challenges:** See challenges as opportunities for growth.
- **Perseverance:** Don't give up easily. Keep pushing forward.
- **Support:** Seek support when needed and offer it to others.

Life:

- **Setbacks:** Learn from setbacks and failures. They are stepping stones to success.
- **Strength:** Cultivate mental and emotional strength.
- **Recovery:** Take time to recover and recharge when needed.

Party:

- **Disasters:** Handle party mishaps with grace and humour.
- **Spirit:** Keep the party spirit alive, no matter the circumstances.
- **Bounce Back:** Always have a backup plan. Adapt and keep the fun going.

Commandment XVI: Thou Shalt Prioritize Self-Care

Work:

- **Breaks:** Take regular breaks to avoid burnout.
- **Boundaries:** Set clear boundaries to maintain a healthy work–life balance.

- **Health:** Prioritize your physical and mental health.

Life:

- **Relaxation:** Make time for relaxation and leisure activities.
- **Health:** Eat well, exercise regularly, and get enough sleep.
- **Mindfulness:** Practise mindfulness and stress-relief techniques.

Party:

- **Preparation:** Ensure you're well-rested and hydrated before the party.
- **Balance:** Enjoy the party but listen to your body's needs.
- **Recovery:** Take care of yourself the day after the party. Rest and recuperate.

Commandment XVII: Thou Shalt Nurture Relationships

Work:

- **Colleagues:** Build strong relationships with your colleagues.
- **Networking:** Connect with professionals in your field.
- **Mentorship:** Seek mentors and be a mentor to others.

Life:

- **Family:** Spend quality time with your family.
- **Friends:** Cultivate and cherish your friendships.
- **Community:** Be an active part of your community.

Party:

- **Inclusivity:** Make sure everyone feels included and valued.
- **Connections:** Facilitate connections between guests.
- **Follow-up:** Keep in touch with new friends made at parties.

Commandment XVIII: Thou Shalt Plan Ahead

Work:

- **Goals:** Set clear goals and plan how to achieve them.
- **Projects:** Plan your projects and tasks ahead of time.
- **Deadlines:** Meet deadlines by planning your time effectively.

Life:

- **Future:** Plan for the future but live in the present.
- **Events:** Plan personal events and activities in advance.
- **Savings:** Plan your finances and save for the future.

Party:

- **Preparation:** Plan every aspect of your party.
- **Supplies:** Ensure you have all necessary supplies ahead of time.
- **Activities:** Plan a variety of activities to keep guests entertained.

Commandment XIX: Thou Shalt Have Integrity

Work:

- **Ethics:** Uphold high ethical standards in all your professional dealings.
- **Honesty:** Be honest and transparent.
- **Trust:** Build trust with your colleagues and clients.

Life:

- **Values:** Live by your values and principles.
- **Honesty:** Be truthful in your interactions.
- **Respect:** Earn respect through integrity and character.

Party:

- **Honesty:** Be honest with your guests. Don't promise what you can't deliver.
- **Respect:** Respect your guests and their belongings.
- **Fairness:** Ensure fair play in all party games and activities.

Commandment XX: Thou Shalt Give Back

Work:

- **Volunteering:** Participate in company-sponsored volunteer activities.
- **Mentorship:** Mentor and help others in your field.
- **Contributions:** Contribute to company initiatives and charity drives.

Life:

- **Charity:** Donate time, money or skills to charitable causes.
- **Kindness:** Practise random acts of kindness.
- **Community:** Get involved in your community and make a difference.

Party:

- **Charity Events:** Host parties for a cause.
- **Sharing:** Share your resources and hospitality generously.
- **Support:** Support friends and family in their endeavors.

Commandment XXI: Thou Shalt Stay Organized

Work:

- **Desk:** Keep your workspace tidy.

- **Calendar:** Use a calendar to keep track of tasks and deadlines.
- **Files:** Organize your files for easy access.

Life:

- **Home:** Maintain a clean and organized home.
- **Schedule:** Keep a personal schedule to manage your time.
- **Documents:** Organize important documents and keep them safe.

Party:

- **Planning:** Plan your party details in advance.
- **Supplies:** Keep party supplies organized and accessible.
- **Flow:** Ensure a smooth flow of activities during the party.

Commandment XXII: Thou Shalt Foster Positive Energy

Work:

- **Attitude:** Maintain a positive attitude.
- **Encouragement:** Encourage and uplift your colleagues.
- **Environment:** Create a positive work environment.

Life:

- **Optimism:** Look on the bright side of life.
- **Energy:** Surround yourself with positive people.
- **Joy:** Spread joy and positivity wherever you go.

Party:

- **Vibes:** Create a positive and welcoming party atmosphere.
- **Fun:** Focus on fun and enjoyment.
- **Encouragement:** Encourage everyone to have a good time.

Commandment XXIII: Thou Shalt Practise Patience

Work:

- **Deadlines:** Be patient with project timelines.
- **Growth:** Understand that growth takes time.
- **Colleagues:** Be patient with colleagues and their learning curves.

Life:

- **Goals:** Patience with long-term goals.
- **Relationships:** Patience in building and maintaining relationships.
- **Challenges:** Patience in overcoming life's challenges.

Party:

- **Preparation:** Patience in party preparations.
- **Guests:** Patience with guests' needs and behaviours.
- **Clean-Up:** Patience in post-party clean-up.

Commandment XXIV: Thou Shalt Be Resourceful

Work:

- **Solutions:** Find creative solutions to problems.
- **Tools:** Use tools and resources effectively.
- **Networking:** Utilize your network for support and opportunities.

Life:

- **Challenges:** Be resourceful when facing life's challenges.
- **Finances:** Be smart with money and resources.

- **Skills:** Develop a diverse skill set.

Party:

- **Decor:** Get creative with party decorations.
- **Budget:** Plan a fun party within your budget.
- **Activities:** Use available resources for entertainment.

Commandment XXV: Thou Shalt Be Adventurous

Work:

- **Projects:** Take on challenging projects.
- **Opportunities:** Seek out new opportunities.
- **Growth:** Step out of your comfort zone for growth.

Life:

- **Travel:** Travel and explore new places.
- **Experiences:** Try new experiences and activities.
- **Risks:** Take calculated risks for personal growth.

Party:

- **Themes:** Experiment with adventurous party themes.
- **Locations:** Host parties in unique and interesting locations.
- **Activities:** Include adventurous activities.

Commandment XXVI: Thou Shalt Cultivate Empathy

Work:

- **Understanding:** Understand your colleagues' perspectives.
- **Support:** Offer support and empathy.
- **Teamwork:** Foster a team environment with empathy.

Life:

- **Compassion:** Show compassion to others.
- **Listening:** Listen empathetically to others.
- **Relationships:** Build relationships on empathy and understanding.

Party:

- **Inclusivity:** Make sure everyone feels included and understood.
- **Support:** Offer support to anyone having a tough time.
- **Kindness:** Show kindness and empathy to all guests.

Commandment XXVII: Thou Shalt Celebrate Diversity

Work:

- **Inclusivity:** Create an inclusive work environment.
- **Learning:** Learn about and respect different cultures and perspectives.
- **Collaboration:** Collaborate with diverse teams.

Life:

- **Cultures:** Celebrate different cultures and traditions.
- **Perspectives:** Embrace diverse perspectives.
- **Friends:** Build a diverse circle of friends.

Party:

- **Themes:** Celebrate diversity through party themes.
- **Food:** Include diverse foods and drinks.
- **Activities:** Incorporate diverse activities and games.

Commandment XXVIII: Thou Shalt Manage Time Wisely

Work:

- **Deadlines:** Meet deadlines through effective time management.
- **Productivity:** Maximize productivity with time management techniques.
- **Priorities:** Prioritize tasks effectively.

Life:

- **Balance:** Balance work, life and leisure.
- **Activities:** Plan activities to make the most of your time.
- **Goals:** Allocate time for personal goals and development.

Party:

- **Schedule:** Plan a schedule for party activities.
- **Pacing:** Pace the party to maintain energy.
- **End:** Know when to end the party.

Commandment XXIX: Thou Shalt Be Accountable

Work:

- **Responsibilities:** Take responsibility for your tasks and actions.
- **Mistakes:** Own up to mistakes and learn from them.
- **Integrity:** Maintain accountability with integrity.

Life:

- **Decisions:** Be accountable for your decisions.
- **Actions:** Take responsibility for your actions.
- **Commitments:** Honour your commitments.

Party:

- **Host:** As a host, be responsible for the party's success.
- **Guests:** Ensure guests are safe and having a good time.
- **Clean-Up:** Take responsibility for post-party clean-up.

Commandment XXX: Thou Shalt Practise Humility

Work:

- **Credit:** Share credit for successes.
- **Learning:** Be open to learning from others.
- **Modesty:** Stay humble, regardless of success.

Life:

- **Gratitude:** Be grateful for what you have.
- **Humbleness:** Stay grounded and humble.
- **Learning:** Learn from everyone you meet.

Party:

- **Modesty:** Be modest and don't boast.
- **Gratitude:** Thank guests for their presence.
- **Enjoyment:** Focus on everyone's enjoyment, not just your own.

Commandment XXXI: Thou Shalt Seek Balance

Work:

- **Workload:** Manage your workload to avoid burnout.
- **Breaks:** Take regular breaks.
- **Boundaries:** Set boundaries to maintain balance.

Life:

- **Priorities:** Balance your priorities.
- **Health:** Balance physical and mental health.
- **Leisure:** Make time for leisure activities.

Party:

- **Activities:** Balance different activities to keep the party interesting.
- **Energy:** Balance high-energy and relaxed moments.
- **Guests:** Balance the needs and desires of different guests.

Commandment XXXII: Thou Shalt Be Honest

Work:

- **Transparency:** Maintain transparency in your work.
- **Feedback:** Provide honest feedback.
- **Ethics:** Uphold ethical standards.

Life:

- **Truthfulness:** Be truthful in your interactions.
- **Integrity:** Live with integrity.
- **Trust:** Build trust through honesty.

Party:

- **Invitations:** Be honest in your invitations and expectations.
- **Feedback:** Provide honest feedback about the party.
- **Games:** Ensure fair play in party games.

Commandment XXXIII: Thou Shalt Be Innovative

Work:

- **Ideas:** Encourage and develop new ideas.
- **Processes:** Innovate work processes for efficiency.
- **Projects:** Take on innovative projects.

Life:

- **Solutions:** Find innovative solutions to problems.
- **Hobbies:** Be innovative in your hobbies and interests.
- **Learning:** Learn new and innovative skills.

Party:

- **Decor:** Innovate with party decorations.
- **Games:** Create new and exciting party games.
- **Themes:** Experiment with unique party themes.

Commandment XXXIV: Thou Shalt Practise Forgiveness

Work:

- **Mistakes:** Forgive mistakes and learn from them.
- **Conflicts:** Resolve conflicts through forgiveness.
- **Growth:** Allow for growth through forgiveness.

Life:

- **Relationships:** Foster healthy relationships through forgiveness.
- **Self:** Forgive yourself for past mistakes.
- **Peace:** Find inner peace through forgiveness.

Party:

- **Mishaps:** Forgive party mishaps and move on.
- **Conflicts:** Resolve party conflicts with forgiveness.
- **Fun:** Focus on fun, not faults.

Commandment XXXV: Thou Shalt Be Proactive

Work:

- **Initiative:** Take initiative in projects and tasks.
- **Planning:** Plan ahead to avoid last-minute rushes.
- **Opportunities:** Seek out and create opportunities.

Life:

- **Goals:** Set and work towards personal goals.
- **Health:** Be proactive about your health.
- **Relationships:** Take proactive steps to maintain relationships.

Party:

- **Preparation:** Prepare proactively for the party.
- **Activities:** Plan activities ahead of time.
- **Backup:** Have a backup plan in case of mishaps.

Commandment XXXVI: Thou Shalt Encourage Others

Work:

- **Support:** Offer support and encouragement to colleagues.
- **Recognition:** Recognize and celebrate others' achievements.
- **Motivation:** Motivate others to achieve their best.

Life:

- **Friends:** Encourage your friends in their endeavors.
- **Family:** Support and encourage your family.
- **Community:** Encourage and uplift your community.

Party:

- **Guests:** Encourage guests to participate and have fun.
- **Games:** Motivate everyone to join in on the games.
- **Atmosphere:** Create an encouraging and supportive atmosphere.

Commandment XXXVII: Thou Shalt Respect Differences

Work:

- **Cultures:** Respect different cultures and perspectives.
- **Ideas:** Be open to different ideas and approaches.
- **Individuals:** Respect individuality in the workplace.

Life:

- **Diversity:** Celebrate diversity in all forms.
- **Opinions:** Respect others' opinions, even if they differ from yours.
- **Cultures:** Embrace and learn from different cultures.

Party:

- **Guests:** Respect the differences among your guests.
- **Themes:** Celebrate diversity through party themes.
- **Food:** Offer diverse food options to cater to all tastes.

Commandment XXXVIII: Thou Shalt Remain Humble

Work:

- **Recognition:** Accept recognition humbly.
- **Learning:** Be open to learning from everyone.
- **Success:** Stay humble in the face of success.

Life:

- **Gratitude:** Practise gratitude daily.
- **Ego:** Keep your ego in check.
- **Kindness:** Treat everyone with kindness and respect.

Party:

- **Hosting:** Be a humble and gracious host.
- **Guests:** Make your guests feel valued and appreciated.
- **Enjoyment:** Focus on everyone's enjoyment, not just your own.

Commandment XXXIX: Thou Shalt Cultivate Wisdom

Work:

- **Knowledge:** Seek knowledge and understanding.
- **Experience:** Learn from your experiences and those of others.
- **Mentorship:** Seek and offer mentorship.

Life:

- **Learning:** Never stop learning.
- **Reflection:** Reflect on your experiences and learn from them.
- **Growth:** Strive for personal growth and wisdom.

Party:

- **Stories:** Share wisdom and stories with guests.
- **Games:** Include games that encourage thinking and learning.
- **Conversations:** Foster meaningful and wise conversations.

Commandment XL: Thou Shalt Live Authentically

Work:

- **True Self:** Be true to yourself in your work.
- **Values:** Uphold your values and principles.
- **Integrity:** Maintain integrity in all dealings.

Life:

- **Authenticity:** Live an authentic and genuine life.
- **Honesty:** Be honest with yourself and others.
- **Passions:** Follow your passions and dreams.

Party:

- **Realness:** Be real and genuine with your guests.
- **Joy:** Find joy in authentic experiences.
- **Connections:** Foster authentic connections with others.

Embrace these commandments to navigate work, life and parties with joy, success and harmony, creating a balanced and fulfilling existence.

17

Extroverts, Introverts and Productivity

If you're walking down the right path and you're willing to keep walking, eventually you'll make progress.

—Barack Obama

The concepts of extroversion and introversion have long fascinated psychologists, sociologists and organizational behaviourists. Understanding these personality types provides profound insights into human behaviour, productivity, and interpersonal dynamics. This chapter delves deep into how extroverts and introverts navigate life and job productivity, supported by real-life examples and psychological theories.

The Dichotomy of Personality: Extroversion and Introversion

Introduction to Personality Dimensions

In personality psychology, two fundamental dimensions often discussed are extroversion and introversion. These dimensions, first popularized by Carl Jung and later elaborated by various psychologists, describe how individuals interact with the world around them. Understanding these traits not only provides insights into personal behaviour but also aids in improving interpersonal relationships and personal well-being.

Extroversion: The Outward-Facing Trait

Characteristics of Extroversion

Extroversion is characterized by a preference for external stimulation. Extroverts are typically outgoing, energetic and thrive in social situations. They are often seen as the life of the party, drawing energy from interactions with others. This personality trait encompasses a range of behaviours and attitudes that make extroverts uniquely equipped to handle and enjoy social environments.

1. **Social Engagement**: Extroverts find social gatherings stimulating and are often the centre of attention. They enjoy meeting new people, engaging in conversations, and are generally very approachable.
2. **High Energy Levels**: Extroverts exhibit high levels of energy and enthusiasm, especially when they are around people. This energy often translates into an active lifestyle, with extroverts participating in various social and physical activities.
3. **Expressiveness**: Extroverts are expressive with their emotions and thoughts. They are more likely to share their feelings and ideas openly, making them appear more transparent and relatable to others.
4. **Leadership**: Due to their outgoing nature, extroverts often find themselves in leadership roles. Their ability to communicate effectively and motivate others makes them natural leaders in group settings.
5. **Risk-Taking**: Extroverts are generally more inclined to take risks. Their comfort with new experiences and their confidence in social situations often lead them to embrace opportunities that others might shy away from.

Biological and Psychological Basis of Extroversion

The preference for external stimulation in extroverts can be traced back to both biological and psychological factors. Research has shown that extroverts tend to have a more active dopamine system, the neurotransmitter associated with reward and pleasure. This heightened dopamine activity makes extroverts more responsive to external rewards, leading them to seek out social interactions and novel experiences.

Psychologically, extroverts often exhibit a positive affect, meaning they experience and express positive emotions more frequently than negative ones. This positive affectivity reinforces their outgoing behaviour, as they associate social interactions with positive outcomes.

Introversion: The Inward-Facing Trait

Characteristics of Introversion

Introversion, on the other hand, is marked by a preference for internal thoughts and feelings over external stimuli. Introverts are usually reserved, enjoy solitary activities, and need time alone to recharge after social interactions. This personality trait includes several distinctive behaviours and attitudes that set introverts apart.

1. **Solitude Preference**: Introverts find comfort in solitude and often seek out time alone to process their thoughts and recharge. They enjoy solitary activities such as reading, writing, and engaging in creative pursuits.
2. **Thoughtfulness**: Introverts are often deep thinkers who reflect extensively on their experiences and ideas. They tend to be more introspective and are skilled at understanding their inner worlds.

3. **Selective Social Interactions**: While introverts do enjoy social interactions, they prefer smaller, more intimate gatherings over large parties. They build deep, meaningful relationships with a few individuals rather than having a large social circle.
4. **Reserved Nature**: Introverts are generally more reserved and may come across as quiet or shy. They tend to listen more than they speak, often providing thoughtful and measured responses in conversations.
5. **Energy Management**: Social interactions, especially in large groups, can be draining for introverts. They require time alone to replenish their energy, which is why they might retreat from social activities more frequently than extroverts.

Biological and Psychological Basis of Introversion

The preference for internal thoughts and feelings in introverts is also rooted in biological and psychological factors. Introverts tend to have a less active dopamine system, making them less driven by external rewards and more focused on internal satisfaction. Additionally, the frontal cortex of introverts, responsible for decision-making and planning, is often more active, indicating a higher level of internal processing.

Psychologically, introverts are more sensitive to environmental stimuli, which can lead to overstimulation in social settings. This sensitivity necessitates a balance between social engagement and solitary time, allowing introverts to manage their energy effectively.

The Spectrum of Extroversion and Introversion

It is important to note that extroversion and introversion are not binary opposites but rather exist on a spectrum. Most individuals exhibit traits of both, with one tendency being more dominant.

This concept, known as ambiversion, reflects the fluidity of human personality and the ability to adapt to different social contexts.

Ambiversion: The Middle Ground

Ambiverts possess a balance of extroverted and introverted traits, allowing them to adapt their behaviour based on the situation. They can enjoy social interactions and also value their alone time. This flexibility often makes ambiverts well-rounded individuals who can navigate various social environments with ease.

1. **Adaptive Social Behaviour**: Ambiverts can be outgoing and sociable in group settings, but they can also appreciate and seek solitude when needed. This adaptability makes them versatile in social situations.
2. **Balanced Energy**: Ambiverts have a balanced approach to energy management. They are not easily overwhelmed by social interactions but also recognize the importance of recharging in solitude.
3. **Effective Communication**: Ambiverts often excel in communication as they can engage in deep, meaningful conversations and also participate in light-hearted, social banter. This makes them effective communicators in both personal and professional settings.
4. **Emotional Regulation**: Ambiverts tend to have good emotional regulation skills. They can express their emotions when appropriate and also maintain composure, making them emotionally stable individuals.

Practical Implications of Understanding Extroversion and Introversion

Understanding whether one is more extroverted or introverted can have significant implications for personal development, career choices, and relationship dynamics.

1. **Personal Development**: Knowing one's dominant personality trait can aid in personal growth. Extroverts can work on enhancing their reflective abilities, while introverts can practise stepping out of their comfort zones in social settings.
2. **Career Choices**: Certain careers are better suited to specific personality traits. Extroverts might thrive in roles that require constant interaction, such as sales or public relations, while introverts might excel in careers that allow for deep focus and solitary work, such as writing or research.
3. **Relationship Dynamics**: Understanding personality traits can improve relationship dynamics. For example, extroverts in a relationship with introverts can learn to respect their partner's need for alone time, while introverts can appreciate the social energy extroverts bring into the relationship.
4. **Mental Health**: Recognizing one's need for social interaction or solitude can play a crucial role in maintaining mental health. Extroverts need to ensure they have ample opportunities for social engagement, while introverts should prioritize time for self-reflection and recharge.

Extroversion and introversion represent two ends of a personality spectrum, each with unique characteristics and implications for behaviour, social interactions and personal well-being. Understanding these traits allows individuals to navigate their social worlds more effectively, fostering better relationships and personal growth. As research continues to evolve, the nuances of these personality dimensions will further illuminate the complexities of human behaviour and the diverse ways people experience and interact with the world.

Productivity in the Workplace

Extroverts in the Workplace:

- **Strengths:** Extroverts excel in roles that require frequent interaction, teamwork and networking. Their ability to engage with others makes them effective in sales, marketing and leadership positions. They are often seen as motivators, bringing enthusiasm and energy to the workplace.
- **Challenges:** However, extroverts may struggle with tasks that require deep concentration or prolonged periods of solitude. Their need for social interaction can sometimes be a distraction, leading to a potential decrease in productivity when working independently.

Introverts in the Workplace:

- **Strengths:** Introverts often thrive in roles that require attention to detail, analytical thinking, and creativity. They excel in research, writing and technical positions where deep focus and solitude are valued. Introverts are also known for their ability to listen and think critically before speaking, which can lead to thoughtful and well-considered contributions.
- **Challenges:** Introverts may find it challenging to engage in networking or large group activities. They may also struggle in environments that require constant social interaction, which can be draining and impact their overall productivity.

Real-Life Examples

Extroverts:

1. **Richard Branson:** The founder of Virgin Group, Branson is a quintessential extrovert. His charisma and ability to

connect with people have been pivotal in building his business empire. Branson's extroverted nature allows him to thrive in high-stakes negotiations and public-speaking engagements, driving his productivity and success.
2. **Oprah Winfrey:** Oprah's success as a talk show host and media mogul is largely due to her extroverted personality. Her ability to engage with guests and audiences has made her one of the most influential figures in media. Oprah's extroversion helps her build strong relationships, crucial for her multifaceted career.

Introverts:

1. **Bill Gates:** As the co-founder of Microsoft, Gates is known for his introverted nature. His ability to focus deeply on complex problems has been a key factor in his success. Gates often highlights how his introversion has allowed him to dedicate time to thinking and innovation, crucial for driving technological advancements.
2. **J.K. Rowling:** The author of the Harry Potter series, Rowling is an introvert who has spoken about how her solitary nature allowed her to create the intricate world of Hogwarts. Her ability to work independently and focus deeply on her writing has been instrumental in her success as an author.

Balancing Productivity: Strategies for Extroverts and Introverts

For Extroverts:

1. **Structured Social Interaction:** Scheduling specific times for social activities can help extroverts maintain focus during

solitary tasks. For example, Branson ensures he has time for meetings and interactions but also schedules time for strategic thinking alone.
2. **Collaborative Environments:** Extroverts thrive in team settings. Creating collaborative workspaces can enhance their productivity and job satisfaction.
3. **Breaks for Interaction:** Taking short breaks to interact with colleagues can recharge extroverts, helping them stay energized throughout the day.

For Introverts:

1. **Quiet Workspaces:** Providing quiet areas where introverts can work without distractions can significantly boost their productivity. Gates often works in secluded environments to maintain his focus.
2. **Scheduled Interaction:** Introverts can benefit from scheduling social interactions to avoid feeling overwhelmed. Rowling, for instance, sets aside specific times for book signings and public engagements.
3. **Leverage Technology:** Tools like email and instant messaging can help introverts communicate effectively without the stress of face-to-face interactions.

The Impact of Remote Work

The rise of remote work has highlighted the differences in how extroverts and introverts approach productivity.

Extroverts:

- **Pros:** Remote work allows extroverts to engage in social activities outside of work hours, maintaining their need for interaction while focusing during work hours.

- **Cons:** The lack of in-person interaction can be challenging. Extroverts may struggle with feelings of isolation, which can impact their motivation and productivity.

Introverts:

- **Pros:** Remote work environments often suit introverts well, providing the solitude they need to concentrate. Introverts can create a workspace tailored to their needs, enhancing their productivity.
- **Cons:** The lack of spontaneous interaction can limit opportunities for introverts to network and build relationships, which are important for career growth.

Productivity, a crucial aspect of both personal and professional life, is deeply influenced by psychological factors. Among these, personality traits play a significant role in determining how individuals approach and manage their tasks. Various psychological theories provide insights into the interplay between personality and productivity, shedding light on why some people thrive in social settings while others excel in solitary environments. This extensive discussion will explore three major psychological theories—Eysenck's Theory of Personality, the Big Five Personality Traits and Mihaly Csikszentmihalyi's Flow Theory—illustrating their concepts with examples of famous individuals to contextualize these ideas in real-world scenarios.

Eysenck's Theory of Personality

The Concept

Hans Eysenck, a pioneering psychologist, proposed a theory that extroversion and introversion are linked to the levels of cortical arousal in the brain. According to Eysenck, extroverts have lower levels of arousal, which drives them to seek external stimulation to raise their arousal levels to an optimal state. Conversely, introverts have higher levels of cortical arousal, leading them to avoid excessive stimulation to maintain their comfort zone.

Extroversion and Productivity

Extroverts, with their inherent need for external stimulation, often find themselves drawn to environments that offer ample opportunities for social interaction. This preference significantly impacts their productivity. Extroverts tend to thrive in dynamic, collaborative settings where they can engage with others and receive immediate feedback. Examples of famous extroverts include:

1. **Oprah Winfrey**: As a highly successful talk show host, media executive, and philanthropist, Oprah exemplifies extroversion. Her ability to connect with people, engage in meaningful conversations, and inspire audiences around the world demonstrates how extroversion can fuel productivity in roles that require high levels of social interaction.
2. **Richard Branson**: The founder of the Virgin Group, Richard Branson is known for his adventurous spirit and charismatic personality. His extroverted nature has played a crucial role in his entrepreneurial success, as he thrives on networking, public speaking, and leading his diverse team of professionals.

Introversion and Productivity

Introverts, on the other hand, excel in environments that allow for deep focus and minimal external stimulation. Their productivity peaks when they can work independently or in small, controlled settings. Examples of famous introverts include:

1. **J.K. Rowling**: The author of the Harry Potter series, J.K. Rowling, is a quintessential introvert. Her ability to create intricate, imaginative worlds and develop complex characters stems from her preference for solitary work, where she can concentrate deeply without external distractions.
2. **Bill Gates**: The co-founder of Microsoft, Bill Gates, is another prominent introvert. His preference for solitary tasks and deep thinking has been a driving force behind his innovative ideas and successful ventures. Gates often retreats to think and reflect, which has contributed to his ability to revolutionize the tech industry.

The Big Five Personality Traits

The Concept

The Big Five Personality Traits model, also known as the Five Factor Model (FFM), is a widely accepted framework for understanding personality. It includes five dimensions: extroversion, agreeableness, conscientiousness, neuroticism and openness to experience. Extroversion and introversion form one of these key dimensions, significantly influencing job performance and satisfaction.

Extroversion in the Workplace

Research has shown that extroverts tend to perform better in roles that require social interaction, teamwork, and communication. They are often enthusiastic, assertive and enjoy being in leadership positions. Famous extroverts who exemplify this include:

1. **Ellen DeGeneres**: As a television host, comedian, and actress, Ellen DeGeneres thrives on social interaction. Her extroverted personality enables her to connect with her

audience, engage guests, and create a lively and entertaining atmosphere on her show.

2. **Barack Obama**: The former president of the United States, Barack Obama, is known for his charismatic and extroverted nature. His ability to engage with the public, deliver compelling speeches, and foster relationships with international leaders highlights how extroversion can be a valuable trait in political leadership.

Introversion in the Workplace

Introverts, conversely, excel in tasks that require deep focus, analytical thinking, and independent work. They often prefer roles that allow for minimal social interaction and more solitary work environments. Examples of successful introverts in the workplace include:

1. **Albert Einstein**: The theoretical physicist, Albert Einstein, is an iconic example of an introvert who made groundbreaking contributions to science through solitary work. His introspective nature and preference for quiet contemplation were instrumental in developing the theory of relativity.
2. **Mark Zuckerberg**: The co-founder and CEO of Facebook, Mark Zuckerberg, is known for his introverted and analytical approach to leadership. His ability to focus on complex problems and innovate within the tech industry showcases the strengths of introversion in the workplace.

Flow Theory

The Concept

Mihaly Csikszentmihalyi's flow theory suggests that people are most productive when they are fully immersed in an activity that matches their skill level. This state of flow, often described as being "in the zone," occurs when individuals experience a balance between the challenge of the task and their abilities, leading to heightened focus and enjoyment.

Extroverts and Flow

Extroverts are more likely to experience flow in social settings where they can engage with others and participate in dynamic activities. Their preference for external stimulation makes collaborative environments ideal for achieving flow. Examples of extroverts who have experienced flow in their careers include:

1. **Tony Robbins**: The motivational speaker and self-help author, Tony Robbins, often describes being in a state of flow during his high-energy seminars and workshops. His ability to captivate and inspire large audiences is a testament to the extroverted experience of flow.
2. **Lady Gaga**: The pop star and actress, Lady Gaga, embodies extroversion through her performances. She frequently enters a state of flow while on stage, fully immersed in her music and interactions with the audience, leading to captivating and powerful performances.

Introverts and Flow

Introverts, on the other hand, are more likely to achieve flow during solitary tasks that require deep concentration and introspection. Their preference for internal stimulation and reflective activities makes these environments conducive to experiencing flow. Examples of introverts who have achieved flow include:

1. **Stephen King**: The prolific author Stephen King often describes the experience of flow while writing. His deep immersion in the creative process, away from distractions,

allows him to produce numerous best-selling novels.
2. **Isaac Newton**: The mathematician and physicist, Isaac Newton, exemplified the introverted experience of flow through his groundbreaking work in mathematics and physics. His solitary study and intense focus led to significant scientific discoveries, including the laws of motion and universal gravitation.

Practical Applications of These Theories

Understanding the interplay between personality traits and productivity can significantly enhance both individual and organizational performance. Here are some practical applications:

1. **Personal Development**: Individuals can leverage their understanding of extroversion and introversion to optimize their productivity. Extroverts can seek out collaborative projects and networking opportunities, while introverts can create environments that minimize distractions and allow for deep work.
2. **Career Choices**: Aligning career paths with personality traits can lead to greater job satisfaction and performance. Extroverts might pursue careers in sales, public relations or entertainment, while introverts might find fulfillment in research, writing or technical fields.
3. **Team Dynamics**: Organizations can build more effective teams by recognizing and balancing extroverted and introverted traits. Extroverts can lead brainstorming sessions and client interactions, while introverts can focus on detailed planning and execution.
4. **Workplace Design**: Creating workspaces that cater to both extroverts and introverts can enhance overall productivity. This might include open areas for collaboration and quiet zones for focused work.

5. **Leadership Strategies**: Leaders can tailor their management approaches to accommodate different personality traits. For example, providing extroverts with opportunities for public recognition and offering introverts time for individual contributions can maximize team performance.

Extroversion and introversion are fundamental dimensions of personality that significantly influence productivity. Through the lens of Eysenck's Theory of Personality, the Big Five Personality Traits and Flow Theory, we can better understand how these traits impact behaviour and performance. By considering examples of famous individuals who embody these traits, we gain practical insights into how to harness the strengths of both extroverts and introverts in various contexts. Understanding these psychological theories allows for a more nuanced approach to personal development, career planning and organizational management, ultimately leading to enhanced productivity and well-being.

Integrating Extroverts and Introverts in Teams

Effective teams often include a mix of extroverts and introverts. Balancing these personality types can lead to a more dynamic and productive team environment.

For Extroverts:

- **Team Roles:** Assign roles that leverage their social skills, such as project management, client interaction or team leadership.
- **Brainstorming Sessions:** Encourage extroverts to lead brainstorming sessions, where their energy can stimulate creative thinking.

For Introverts:

- **Individual Tasks:** Assign tasks that require deep concentration and analytical skills, such as research, writing or technical development.
- **Silent Meetings:** Incorporate silent meetings where team members write down their ideas before discussing them, giving introverts time to process and contribute.

Real-Life Organizational Examples

Google: Google's workplace culture is designed to cater to both extroverts and introverts. They offer open office spaces for collaboration, as well as quiet pods and private rooms for focused work. This balance helps all employees perform at their best.

Buffer: Buffer, a social media management company, has a remote work culture that supports both personality types. They provide flexibility for employees to work in environments that suit them best, whether it's a bustling coffee shop or a quiet home office. Buffer also encourages asynchronous communication, allowing introverts to contribute thoughtfully.

Understanding the dynamics of extroversion and introversion is crucial for optimizing productivity in both life and the workplace. By recognizing and accommodating the unique strengths and challenges of each personality type, individuals and organizations can create environments that foster success and well-being.

The interplay between extroverts and introverts adds a rich layer of diversity to human interaction. Embracing these differences and leveraging them effectively can lead to greater innovation, creativity and productivity. Whether through structured social interaction for extroverts or quiet workspaces for introverts, finding the right balance is key to unlocking the full potential of every individual.

Building Harmonious Relationships: How Introverts, Extroverts and Ambiverts Can Help Each Other

In both personal and professional settings, understanding and leveraging the strengths of introverts, extroverts and ambiverts can create a more harmonious and productive environment. By recognizing the unique contributions each personality type brings, individuals can foster mutual respect, effective communication and collaborative success. This guide will explore ways introverts, extroverts and ambiverts can support each other, including specific strategies, activities and games that promote teamwork and understanding.

How Introverts Can Help Extroverts

Enhancing Focus and Reflection

Introverts excel in environments that require deep thinking and concentration. They can help extroverts by providing insights and techniques for focused work.

1. **Encourage Reflection**: Introverts can gently remind extroverts to take time for reflection. This can be done by suggesting short breaks for contemplation after meetings or brainstorming sessions.
2. **Share Organizational Skills**: Introverts often have well-developed organizational skills. They can assist extroverts in planning and prioritizing tasks, ensuring that extroverts' enthusiasm is channelled effectively.
3. **Create Quiet Workspaces**: Introverts can help design or

suggest quiet areas in the office where extroverts can retreat to concentrate on tasks that require undivided attention.

Facilitating Deep Connections

Introverts value deep, meaningful connections. They can teach extroverts the importance of building such relationships.

1. **Model Deep Conversations**: Introverts can initiate and model deeper conversations, encouraging extroverts to move beyond surface-level interactions.
2. **Mentorship Programmes**: Introverts can participate in mentorship programmes, providing extroverts with a space to develop more profound professional and personal relationships.

How Extroverts Can Help Introverts

Encouraging Social Interaction

Extroverts thrive in social settings and can help introverts become more comfortable in such environments.

1. **Introduce Gradual Socialization**: Extroverts can introduce introverts to social activities gradually, ensuring they do not feel overwhelmed. Starting with smaller groups can help introverts acclimate to social interactions.
2. **Highlight the Benefits of Networking**: Extroverts can share personal stories and benefits of networking, helping introverts see the value in expanding their professional and social circles.
3. **Create Inclusive Activities**: Extroverts can organize inclusive activities that cater to both introverts and extroverts, ensuring that everyone feels comfortable and engaged.

Boosting Confidence

Extroverts often exude confidence, which can be contagious and beneficial for introverts.

1. **Provide Positive Reinforcement**: Extroverts can offer genuine compliments and positive feedback to introverts, helping to build their confidence in social and professional settings.
2. **Encourage Public Speaking**: Extroverts can encourage introverts to participate in public speaking opportunities, starting with small, supportive groups.

How Ambiverts Can Help Both Introverts and Extroverts

Bridging the Gap

Ambiverts naturally balance the traits of both introverts and extroverts. They can play a crucial role in bridging the gap between the two personality types.

1. **Facilitate Communication**: Ambiverts can act as intermediaries, helping introverts and extroverts understand each other's perspectives and communication styles.
2. **Adapt to Situations**: Ambiverts can adjust their behaviour to suit different social contexts, providing a model for both introverts and extroverts on how to navigate varying levels of social interaction.
3. **Mediate Conflicts**: In the event of misunderstandings or conflicts, ambiverts can mediate by leveraging their balanced approach to address concerns and find mutually acceptable solutions.

Enhancing Team Dynamics

Ambiverts' ability to thrive in both social and solitary settings makes them valuable team members who can enhance overall team dynamics.

1. **Encourage Collaboration**: Ambiverts can encourage collaboration by creating opportunities for both introverts and extroverts to contribute their strengths in a team setting.
2. **Model Flexibility**: By demonstrating flexibility in their interactions, ambiverts can show introverts and extroverts how to adapt their behaviour to different situations, fostering a more cohesive team environment.

Collaborative Activities and Games

To foster better understanding and teamwork between introverts, extroverts and ambiverts, various activities and games can be played in both office and home settings.

Office Activities

1. **Brainstorming Sessions**: Structured brainstorming sessions where everyone is given time to speak. Introverts can contribute their well-thought-out ideas, while extroverts can drive the energy and enthusiasm, and ambiverts can bridge the gap by facilitating balanced participation.
2. **Role Reversal Workshops**: Periodic workshops where introverts, extroverts and ambiverts switch roles. Introverts lead discussions or presentations, while extroverts engage in tasks that require deep focus and reflection. Ambiverts can help moderate and provide support.
3. **Feedback Circles**: Regular feedback sessions where team members share constructive feedback. This helps

extroverts learn the value of reflective thinking, introverts practise articulating their thoughts openly, and ambiverts enhance their role as intermediaries.

4. **Team-Building Games**:
   o **Two Truths and a Lie**: A game where each person states three statements about themselves—two truths and one lie. Others guess which is the lie. This helps in building rapport and understanding.
   o **Pictionary**: A drawing and guessing game that encourages creativity and teamwork.
   o **Escape Rooms**: Team-based problem-solving activities that require both social interaction and focused thinking.

Home Activities

1. **Book Clubs**: Organize a book club where both introverts, extroverts and ambiverts can share their perspectives. Introverts can prepare their thoughts in advance, extroverts can drive the discussions, and ambiverts can facilitate balanced participation.
2. **Game Nights**: Host game nights with a mix of interactive and strategy games.
   o **Charades**: Encourages extroverts to showcase their expressive skills and introverts to step out of their comfort zone in a fun setting. Ambiverts can help manage the game's pace and engagement.
   o **Settlers of Catan**: A strategy board game that requires negotiation and planning, catering to all personality types.
3. **Cooking Together**: Cooking as a group activity where extroverts can enjoy the social aspect, introverts can focus

on the detailed process of cooking, and ambiverts can facilitate cooperation.
4. **Hiking and Nature Walks**: Organize nature walks or hiking trips. These activities allow extroverts to enjoy the social company, introverts to appreciate the tranquility of nature, and ambiverts to balance group dynamics.

Strategies for Better Understanding

Communication Techniques

1. **Active Listening**: All personality types can practise active listening. Extroverts can focus on listening more and talking less, introverts can work on expressing their thoughts clearly, and ambiverts can model effective listening and speaking balance.
2. **Regular Check Ins**: Schedule regular check ins to discuss how each person feels about their interactions. This helps in addressing any discomfort and improving mutual understanding.
3. **Shared Goals**: Establish shared goals that require both social interaction and deep thinking. Working towards a common objective can highlight the strengths of all personality types.

Environmental Adjustments

1. **Flexible Workspaces**: Design flexible workspaces that cater to introverts, extroverts and ambiverts. Include quiet areas for focused work and open spaces for collaboration.
2. **Flexible Schedules**: Allow for flexible work schedules where introverts can have alone time to work on deep

tasks, extroverts can engage in collaborative projects, and ambiverts can adjust their work style as needed.
3. **Balanced Workload**: Ensure a balanced workload that includes tasks suited for all personality types. Extroverts can take on roles that require interaction, introverts can handle tasks that require detailed attention, and ambiverts can manage a mix of both.

Building a harmonious relationship between introverts, extroverts and ambiverts requires mutual understanding, respect and the willingness to learn from each other. By recognizing and leveraging each other's strengths, all personality types can create a more productive and positive environment. Whether in the office or at home, engaging in collaborative activities and games, practising effective communication, and making thoughtful environmental adjustments can significantly enhance the interactions and productivity of introverts, extroverts and ambiverts alike.

18

Revise and Refresh Your Mojo

*Success is the sum of small efforts,
repeated day in and day out.*

—Robert Collier

1. Embracing Singular Concentration

Understanding the Core Concept: Dive deep into the essence of focusing on a singular goal that simplifies or eliminates other tasks. Discuss the evolution of this concept through history and its relevance in today's fast-paced world.

The Science of Focus: Explore the neurological basis of focus, detailing how the brain responds to focused versus scattered attention. Include anecdotes from successful individuals and companies illustrating the transformative power of single-minded concentration.

2. Setting Priorities and Goals

Identifying Your Main Objective: Offer a step-by-step guide to self-reflection and discovery, helping readers pinpoint their most crucial goal. Include exercises, questionnaires and real-life examples.

Crafting SMART Goals: Break down the process of creating Specific, Measurable, Achievable, Relevant and Time-Bound goals with detailed case studies and practical applications.

The Domino Effect: Explain how small, strategic actions can trigger a chain reaction leading to significant outcomes. Use mathematical models and historical examples to illustrate this principle.

3. Mastering Time and Productivity

Time-Blocking Techniques: Provide an in-depth analysis of time-blocking methods, including the Pomodoro Technique and Eisenhower Matrix. Share success stories of individuals and organizations that have mastered these techniques.

Overcoming Procrastination: Discuss the psychological theories behind procrastination and offer advanced strategies to combat it, such as cognitive behavioural techniques and habit formation theories.

The 80/20 Principle: Explore the Pareto Principle in detail, providing statistical data and examples from various industries to show how focusing on the vital few can yield disproportionate results.

4. Cultivating the Right Mindset and Habits

Developing a Growth Mindset: Delve into Carol Dweck's research on growth versus fixed mindsets. Include interviews with professionals who have successfully adopted a growth mindset.

Forming Positive Habits: Present habit formation theories from experts like Charles Duhigg and B.J. Fogg, with actionable steps to integrate these habits into daily life.

Understanding Willpower: Examine the science of willpower, referencing studies by researchers like Roy Baumeister. Offer techniques to conserve and strengthen willpower, such as managing decision fatigue and replenishing energy.

5. Balancing Work and Life

Harmonizing Work and Personal Life: Provide strategies for achieving harmony between professional and personal responsibilities. Include examples of flexible work arrangements and boundary-setting techniques.

The Importance of Rest and Recreation: Discuss the significance of rest, including sleep science and the benefits of leisure activities. Provide practical tips for incorporating restorative practices into daily routines.

6. Implementing and Executing Plans

Creating Action Plans and Milestones: Offer a comprehensive guide to breaking down your main objective into manageable steps and setting milestones. Include project management tools and templates.

Tracking Your Progress: Present various methods for monitoring progress, such as journaling, digital tracking apps, and accountability partnerships.

Accountability and Support: Discuss the role of accountability in achieving goals. Include stories of support networks, mentors and peer groups that have helped individuals stay on track.

7. Overcoming Obstacles

Handling Setbacks: Provide strategies for resilience and adaptability, including techniques from positive psychology and stoicism.

Managing Distractions: Identify common distractions and offer solutions for minimizing them, such as digital detoxes and mindfulness practices.

Maintaining Commitment: Discuss long-term commitment strategies, including goal reinforcement techniques and the role of intrinsic motivation.

8. *Learning from Real-Life Examples*

Success Stories: Present detailed case studies of individuals and companies that achieved extraordinary results by focusing on their main objective. Include diverse examples from different fields.

Lessons from Failures: Analyse failures and challenges faced by these case studies to extract valuable lessons on the importance of focus and perseverance.

9. *Reflecting and Moving Forward*

Reflecting on the Journey: Summarize the key insights and principles discussed. Encourage readers to reflect on their own journey and the impact of focusing on their main objective.

Next Steps: Provide a roadmap for readers to take actionable steps and apply the principles learned. Include resources for further reading and personal development.

10. *Historical and Cultural Insights*

Ancient Wisdom on Focus: Explore how historical figures and ancient cultures understood and applied the power of single-minded focus. Include examples from different civilizations and their impact on modern productivity concepts.

Cultural Approaches to Productivity: Analyse how various cultures approach focus and productivity differently. Include comparisons between Eastern and Western philosophies and their influence on work ethics.

11. Neuroscience and Psychology

The Neuroscience of Focus: Dive into the neurological underpinnings of focus, detailing how different brain regions are activated during concentrated tasks. Include cutting-edge research on the impact of mindfulness and meditation on brain function.

Psychological Barriers: Explore common psychological obstacles to focus, such as anxiety, fear of failure and perfectionism. Provide evidence-based strategies to overcome these barriers.

12. Leveraging Technology

Tech Tools for Focus: Discuss modern tools and apps designed to enhance focus and productivity. Include reviews of popular productivity software and their practical applications.

Digital Detox: Examine the benefits of reducing digital distractions and provide methods for implementing a digital detox. Include interviews with individuals who have successfully unplugged.

13. Personal Growth and Self-Care

Mindfulness and Meditation: Present various mindfulness and meditation practices that enhance mental clarity and concentration. Include guided exercises and testimonials from practitioners.

The Role of Sleep and Nutrition: Discuss the role of sleep and diet in maintaining high levels of focus and energy. Include advice from nutritionists and sleep experts.

14. Creativity and Innovation

Art and Focus: Explore how artists and creatives harness focus to produce their best work. Include interviews with artists and a look into their creative processes.

Creative Problem Solving: Present techniques for applying focused thinking to solve complex problems in innovative ways. Include brainstorming methods and examples from creative fields.

15. Alternative Approaches

Holistic Practices: Examine how practices like yoga, acupuncture, and aromatherapy can enhance focus and reduce stress. Include scientific evidence and personal anecdotes.

Nature's Impact on Focus: Discuss the impact of spending time in nature on mental clarity and productivity. Include research on nature therapy and its benefits.

16. Philosophical and Ethical Perspectives

Philosophy of Focus: Examine philosophical theories related to single-mindedness and purpose. Include discussions on existentialism and stoicism.

Ethics of Ambition: Explore the ethical considerations of pursuing personal ambitions. Discuss the balance between individual goals and societal impact.

17. Storytelling and Engagement

Using Narratives: Use stories to illustrate principles of focus and engage readers more deeply. Include fictional and non-fictional stories.

Personal Experiences: Share personal anecdotes and experiences with focus and productivity, including both successes and failures.

18. Building Supportive Communities

Creating Focused Communities: Discuss how to create and maintain a community that supports collective focus and productivity. Include examples of successful communities and their practices.

Social Influence: Examine the impact of social environments on individual focus. Provide strategies for cultivating positive influences.

19. Learning from the Unusual

Uncommon Success Stories: Highlight lesser-known individuals or organizations that have achieved success through focus. Include unique and inspiring stories.

Lessons from Failure: Analyse notable failures to extract lessons on the importance of focus and the consequences of its absence.

20. Spiritual Dimensions

Spiritual Practices for Focus: Explore how spiritual disciplines such as prayer and contemplation can enhance concentration. Include perspectives from different religious traditions.

The Inner Journey: Reflect on the spiritual and existential aspects of focusing on one's purpose. Include philosophical and metaphysical insights.

21. Practical Applications Across Fields

Focus in Sports: Discuss techniques athletes use to achieve peak performance through focus. Include interviews with sports psychologists and athletes.

Focus in Relationships: Apply the principles of focus to improve personal and professional relationships. Include case studies and practical advice.

Embracing Failure and Criticism: Pathways to Growth

Failure and criticism, often seen negatively, can drive personal and professional development. Accepting these experiences as opportunities for growth is crucial. This exploration reveals how various theories and real-life examples can help transform setbacks into success.

Carol Dweck's Growth Mindset Theory suggests that seeing failure as a learning opportunity fosters resilience and a passion for learning, essential for overcoming setbacks. Resilience Theory, supported by Ann Masten, highlights the importance of recovering from adversity with optimism and support. The Iterative Process Model, used in fields like software development, shows that failure is integral to continuous improvement.

Criticism, when viewed as constructive feedback, plays a vital role in growth. The Feedback Loop Theory emphasizes feedback's role in adjusting actions for better outcomes. The Johari Window Model increases self-awareness by uncovering blind spots through feedback. The 360-Degree Feedback Method provides a holistic view of strengths and areas for improvement, enhancing overall performance.

Experimental theories and real-life examples offer practical insights. The Marshmallow Experiment shows the value of delayed gratification, paralleling the patience needed to accept failure and criticism. The Pygmalion Effect demonstrates how higher expectations improve performance when criticism is seen positively. The Rubber Band Theory likens human potential to a rubber band that stretches with challenges, promoting growth.

Strategies for embracing failure and criticism include reframing failure as a learning experience, actively seeking constructive feedback, practising self-compassion, adopting a learning-oriented approach, and developing emotional intelligence. These strategies help individuals reflect, learn and grow from every experience.

The benefits of embracing failure and criticism are numerous. Enhanced resilience helps individuals recover from setbacks and achieve their goals. Continuous improvement fosters a culture of learning and refinement. Increased self-awareness allows for targeted development. Improved relationships result from responding positively to feedback, demonstrating a commitment to growth. Ultimately, embracing failure and criticism leads to long-term success and adaptability.

Failure and criticism are invaluable tools for growth. By seeing failure as a learning opportunity and appreciating constructive feedback, individuals can turn setbacks into stepping stones for success. Embrace failure, welcome criticism, and watch yourself grow into a better, more successful individual.

Embracing Failure and Appreciating Criticism: A Path to Personal and Professional Growth

Failure and criticism, often viewed as negative experiences, can be powerful catalysts for personal and professional growth. Accepting failure and appreciating criticism are essential skills that can transform setbacks into opportunities for improvement. This extensive exploration will delve into various experimental theories and real-life examples to demonstrate how embracing these elements can make you a better and more successful individual.

1. Understanding Failure: Theoretical Perspectives

The Growth Mindset Theory

Carol Dweck's Growth Mindset Theory posits that individuals with a growth mindset perceive failure as a learning opportunity rather than a setback. They believe that abilities and intelligence can be developed through dedication and hard work. This mindset fosters resilience and a passion for learning, which are crucial for overcoming failures and achieving success.

The Resilience Theory

Resilience Theory, supported by the works of psychologists like Ann Masten, emphasizes the ability to recover from adversity. Resilience involves a combination of personal attributes, such as optimism and self-efficacy, and external factors like supportive relationships. Building resilience helps individuals bounce back from failures stronger and more determined.

The Iterative Process Model

The Iterative Process Model, often used in fields like software development and scientific research, involves a cycle of prototyping, testing, analysing and refining. This model highlights that failure is an integral part of the process, leading to continuous improvement. By adopting an iterative approach, individuals can embrace failure as a step toward innovation and excellence.

2. The Role of Criticism: Constructive Feedback for Growth

The Feedback Loop Theory

The Feedback Loop Theory, rooted in cybernetics and systems theory, emphasizes the importance of feedback in self-regulating systems. Constructive criticism acts as feedback, enabling individuals to adjust their actions and strategies. By viewing criticism as valuable input rather than personal attacks, individuals can enhance their performance and achieve better outcomes.

The Johari Window Model

The Johari Window Model, developed by psychologists Joseph Luft and Harrington Ingham, explores self-awareness and mutual understanding. It consists of four quadrants: Open, Hidden, Blind and Unknown. Criticism helps uncover the Blind quadrant—areas others see but we don't. Embracing feedback increases self-awareness and fosters personal growth.

The 360-Degree Feedback Method

The 360-Degree Feedback Method involves receiving feedback from various sources, including peers, subordinates and supervisors. This comprehensive approach provides a holistic view of an individual's strengths and areas for improvement. Appreciating and acting on such feedback leads to well-rounded development and enhanced performance.

3. Experimental Theories and Real-Life Applications

The Marshmallow Experiment

Walter Mischel's Marshmallow Experiment demonstrated the significance of delayed gratification. Children who resisted eating a marshmallow immediately for a promised reward later showed better life outcomes. Similarly, accepting failure and appreciating criticism requires patience and delayed gratification, leading to long-term success.

The Pygmalion Effect

The Pygmalion Effect, or self-fulfilling prophecy, illustrates how higher expectations lead to improved performance. When individuals view criticism as a belief in their potential for growth, they are more likely to rise to the challenge. Embracing criticism with a positive mindset fosters self-improvement and higher achievement.

The Rubber Band Theory

The Rubber Band Theory compares human potential to a rubber band, which stretches when pulled. Failures and criticisms act as the force that stretches the rubber band, pushing individuals out of their comfort zones. The more they stretch, the greater their potential for growth and resilience.

4. Strategies for Embracing Failure and Criticism

Reframing Failure

Reframing involves changing the way we perceive failure. Instead of seeing it as a negative outcome, view it as a valuable learning experience. Reflect on what went wrong, identify lessons learned, and apply these insights to future endeavors.

Seeking Constructive Feedback

Actively seek feedback from trusted sources. Encourage honest and constructive criticism by creating a safe and open environment. Use this feedback to identify blind spots and areas for improvement.

Practising Self-Compassion

Self-compassion, as researched by Kristin Neff, involves treating oneself with kindness and understanding during times of failure. Recognize that failure is a shared human experience and avoid harsh self-judgement. Self-compassion fosters resilience and a growth mindset.

Adopting a Learning-Oriented Approach

Adopt a learning-oriented approach to both success and failure. Celebrate successes as milestones in the learning journey and view failures as stepping stones. Maintain curiosity and a willingness to learn from every experience.

Developing Emotional Intelligence

Emotional intelligence, popularized by Daniel Goleman, involves recognizing and managing one's emotions and understanding others' emotions. High emotional intelligence helps individuals respond to criticism constructively and manage the emotional impact of failure.

5. *Benefits of Embracing Failure and Criticism*

Enhanced Resilience

Embracing failure and criticism builds resilience, enabling individuals to recover quickly from setbacks. Resilient individuals are more likely to persevere and achieve their goals despite challenges.

Continuous Improvement

Accepting failure and valuing criticism fosters a culture of continuous improvement. Individuals who seek feedback and learn from their mistakes are better equipped to refine their skills and strategies.

Increased Self-Awareness

Criticism, when accepted constructively, enhances self-awareness. Understanding one's strengths and weaknesses allows for targeted personal and professional development.

Improved Relationships

Embracing feedback and responding positively to criticism improves interpersonal relationships. It demonstrates humility, openness and a commitment to growth, earning respect and trust from others.

Long-Term Success

Ultimately, the willingness to accept failure and appreciate criticism leads to long-term success. It cultivates a mindset of growth and adaptability, essential for navigating the complexities of life and achieving sustained excellence.

Failure and criticism, though often perceived negatively, are invaluable tools for personal and professional growth. By embracing failure as a learning opportunity and appreciating criticism as constructive feedback, individuals can transform setbacks into stepping stones for success. Through various experimental theories and real-life applications, it becomes evident that these elements are crucial for building resilience, fostering continuous improvement, and achieving long-term success. Embrace failure, welcome criticism, and watch yourself grow into a better, more successful individual.

www.ingramcontent.com/pod-product-compliance
Lightning Source LLC
Chambersburg PA
CBHW032126160426
43197CB00008B/538